MAKING SENSE OUT OF SUFFERING

Making Sense
Out of Suffering

Peter Kreeft

SERVANT BOOKS
Ann Arbor, Michigan

Cover design by Kathleen Schuetz

Published by Servant Books, P.O. Box 8617, Ann Arbor,
Michigan 48107

12   95 94

Printed in the United States of America
ISBN 0-89283-219-3

Contents

Foreword

THIS IS A WISE BOOK. Therefore, it is the thoughts of a wise man. Wisdom and speakers of wisdom are in rather short supply in our civilization. What we have instead are the experts—the experts on the economy, on the atmosphere of Mars, on why aircraft crash, on what is wrong with our body, and on whether the man who pulled the trigger is sane or not. But— have you noticed?—the experts, despite their assured tones, rarely agree with each other; and we, increasingly, don't trust any of them. Still, we are so surrounded by experts, so exposed to their pronouncements in the media, that we are not even very sure of the difference between a wise man and an expert. To be wise is to be discerning between the false and the true, to be balanced in judgement, to be, in fact, very sane. A wise man, indeed, if you can find one, is a good guide amidst the claims of the experts. Socrates was a wise man. He knew how much he didn't know; he was, assuredly, not an expert. Just wise. That is why, after twenty-five centuries, we still ponder his wisdom.

Peter Kreeft is a wise man. *I* say it; he would never say so. I say it, not only on the basis of this wise book but on the basis of more than half a dozen books. Readers who know his *Love Is Stronger than Death* or *Heaven: The Heart's Deepest Longing* already know that what I say is true; and the reader who begins with this book will find it out. There are many writers that I enjoy for their readability or wit or storytelling or knowledge, but there are very few indeed that I should call wise with the confidence that I call Kreeft so.

Here he tackles the hardest subject in the world, the tears and groans of mankind, the existence of pain and suffering, the problem or (what is not at all the same thing) the *mystery* of suffering. The suffering of the innocent, the suffering of the loving. If only villains got broken backs or cancers, if only cheaters and crooks got Parkinson's disease, we should see a sort of celestial justice in the universe (but in that case, of course, no one would care to risk being a villain or a crook). But, as it is, a sweet-tempered child lies dying of a brain tumor, a happy young wife sees her husband and child killed before her eyes by a drunken driver; and in our empathy with the dying boy or the bereft wife and mother we soundlessly scream at the stars, "Why? Why?" A mention of God—of God's will—doesn't help a bit. How could a good God, a loving God, do that? How could he even let it happen? And no answer comes from the indifferent stars.

Long ago when my wife, Davy, still lived, she was deeply impressed by a little story our doctor (himself deeply impressed) told her. It was his painful duty to tell an unsuspecting woman that the x-rays had shown that she had cancer, inoperable cancer. The woman was silent for an instant, and then she said quietly, almost to herself: "Thank God for trusting me with it." How could she have said that? Davy asked. What did she *mean*? It was almost as though that woman knew something, had some understanding, hidden from us. Maybe it was a clue.

I said above that a wise man—only a wise man, not an expert—is a good guide. And it is, precisely, a guide that Peter Kreeft means to be in this book. He guides us among the explanations that other men, experts perhaps, have arrived at to explain the mystery, and shows us where they fall short. He gathers clues. He is all that a guide should be, asking us to use our own eyes, our own discernment—in short, to be wise ourselves. And he invites and allows the reader to talk back, so that the journey is enlivened by patches of brisk Socratic dialog.

The journey is a real one. That is, it starts now when we turn the page, and, if we don't falter, it takes us somewhere. I shall not attempt to say where; after all, this is a foreword, just before the journey begins.

But, having made the journey with our guide myself, I can say that it is a journey well worth making. And I wish you Godspeed.

SHELDON VANAUKEN

ONE

The Problem

"Tell me frankly, I appeal to you—answer me: imagine that it is you yourself who are erecting the edifice of human destiny with the aim of making men happy in the end, of giving them peace and contentment at last, but that to do that it is absolutely necessary, and indeed quite inevitable, to torture to death only one tiny creature, the little girl who beat her breast with her little fist, and to found the edifice on her unavenged tears—would you consent to be the architect on those conditions? Tell me and do not lie!"

Ivan Karamazov

BY THE TIME YOU FINISH READING this book, ten thousand children will starve, four thousand will be brutally beaten by their parents, and one thousand will be raped.

If you took a poll asking who the profoundest thinker of all time was, the man who would probably come out second, after Jesus, is Buddha. Buddha's entire philosophy centers around his answer to the problem of suffering. Whether that philosophy is true or false, here is a man who descended deep, deep into the mystery of suffering. How can we not hear him out?

His name was Gotama Siddhartha. "Buddha" is not a name but a title, like Messiah or Christ. It means "awakened one." He was born a prince, and his father the king kept him in the royal palace for years in order to win him over to the idea of being a king. For there had been prophecies at his birth that this child would become either the greatest king in India's history or the greatest world-denying mystic. Though Gotama's father did all he could to make kingship attractive, Gotama was a curious youth, and one night he bribed the charioteer to drive him outside the palace walls into the city, which his father had forbidden him to see. There he saw the Four Distressing Sights.

The first sight was a sick man. His father had allowed no sickness into the palace. "Why does that man cough and wheeze? Why is his face red?" "He is sick, O lord Gotama." "Can anyone get sick?" "Yes, my lord, even you." "Why do people get sick and suffer so?" "No one knows, O lord Gotama." "That is terrible! I must read this riddle." So Gotama spent the night in fruitless meditation and did not read the riddle of suffering.

The second night, the second ride, the Second Distressing Sight: an old man. His father had allowed no old men into the palace. "Why is that man leaning on a cane? Why is his skin all wrinkled? Why is he so weak?" "He is old, O lord Gotama." "Can anyone get old?" "Yes, my lord, even you will one day be old." "Why do people get old?" "No one knows, O lord Gotama." "That is terrible! I must read this riddle." So Gotama spent a second night in fruitless meditation on two riddles.

The third night, the third ride, the Third Distressing Sight: a dead man. Gotama had never seen such a thing. No motion, no breath, no life. "Why does that man lie so still?" "He is dead, O lord Gotama." "Will he rise again?" "No, lord Gotama." "Can anyone become dead?" "Nay, everyone, my lord. Life's one certainty is that we will all one day die." "Why? Why do we suffer and get old and die?" "No one knows." "Terrible! Terrible! The riddle must be read." But a third night produced no solution to the terrible riddle.

The fourth night, a fourth ride, the Fourth Distressing Sight: a *sanyassin*, an old Hindu mystic and holy man who had renounced the world and sought to purify his soul and find wisdom. An old man with a robe and a begging bowl. "What is that?" "A sanyassin." "What is a sanyassin?" "One who has renounced all worldly possessions." "Why would anyone do that?" "To become wise." "What is it to be wise?" "To understand the great mysteries." "What mysteries?" "Why we suffer, and why we get old and die." "I shall be a sanyassin." And Gotama renounced his princedom and his palace and became a sanyassin.

But the life of asceticism made him no wiser than the life of worldly indulgence, and after fruitless years of this life he decided on the Middle Way: just as much food, sleep, and creature comforts as he needed, no more, no less; neither to indulge nor to torture his body. He took a decent meal for the first time in years, thereby alienating all the other sanyassins except five, who stuck around and became his first disciples. Then he sat under a tree, the sacred Bo tree, or Bodhi tree, in full lotus posture, determined not to rise until he had read the great riddle. When he arose, he proclaimed, "I am Buddha," and enunciated his Four Noble Truths.

The Four Noble Truths are the substance of Buddhism. When a disciple demanded Buddha's answer to other great questions, he reprimanded him; only the Four Noble Truths are needed. They are:

1. That life is suffering (*dukkha*: the word means a bone or axle out of its socket, broken, alienated from itself). We are born in suffering, we live in suffering, we die in suffering. To have what you wish you hadn't, and not to have what you wish you had, is suffering.

2. That the cause of suffering (and here Buddha finally reads his riddle) is desire (*tanha*: greed, craving, selfishness). Desire creates a gap between itself and satisfaction; that gap is suffering.

3. That the way to end suffering is to end desire. *Nirvana* (extinction) is that state. Remove the cause and you remove the effect. The world tries to close the gap between desire and satisfaction by increasing satisfaction, and never succeeds.

Buddha takes the opposite road: decrease desire to zero.

4. That the way to end desire is the Noble Eightfold Path of ego-reduction. Life is divided into eight aspects, and in each of them the disciple practices a gradual releasement, simplification, and purification. It is a total, lifelong task; everything is brought into the service of desire-reduction for the sake of *Nirvana,* the elimination of suffering.

I am not a Buddhist. I cannot help viewing *Nirvana* as spiritual euthanasia, killing the patient (the self, the I, the ego) to cure the disease (egotism, selfishness). Buddhism eliminates the I that hates and suffers, yes; but that is also the I that loves. Compassion (*karuna*) is one of the great Buddhist virtues, but not love (*agape*). Buddha seems to be simply unaware of the possibility of unselfish love, unselfish will, unselfish passion, an unselfish self.

Nevertheless, I cannot help standing in awe of Buddha's own passion to read his great riddle, and equally in awe of his program: nothing less than the transformation of human nature. No one but Jesus ever had a more radical program. And Jesus too placed himself squarely in the middle of the real problem of suffering and gave a radically different solution.

Here is an excerpt from a paper by a student in one of my philosophy classes at Boston College. She titles it simply "Help!"

My twenty-seven-year-old friend can't lift her hand to scratch her nose. She can't move anything but her eyes, mouth and head . . . sort of.

It's been over two years since she started walking into walls. After a while she had to lift her legs by hand in order to position them properly in her car, a flashy black TransAm she loved. Then came the crutches, but the atrophying of her right hand led to the use of a walker. The next thing she knew, she couldn't get around with the walker and her hand became useless. She started using a wheelchair; the car went into storage. Then her other hand started to go, and then her whole body went, and she became bedridden. I can't remember for sure how long this process took, probably because I don't want to remember, but it seems it took about nine months for Elaine to go from bad to worse to hell. Finally the doctors gave in and diagnosed multiple sclerosis.

I, her family, friends, and co-workers watched our friend change from a vibrant, generous, loving young woman to a lump of flesh totally without control, will, or desire. In the beginning I would cry frequently, and dreams of her walking and talking—the old Elaine—constantly haunted my nights. My torment was over the *why* of her condition: for what is she being made to suffer?

I shall never forget reading about the boy in the bubble. I think he was an only child. He had a rare disease (how common rare diseases seem to be!) that necessitated his living his whole life in a sterile plastic bubble. Any touch, a single germ, could kill him. All communication, recreation, education, everything was through the bubble. Finally, he was dying. Since he was doomed anyway, he asked to touch his father's hand—his father, who had loved him and stayed with him all his life. What unspeakable love and pain was in that one touch! I wonder . . . did it feel hot and burning like iron, or soft like a womb?

Rabbi Harold Kushner wrote the best-selling book *When Bad Things Happen to Good People* because he had to understand the tragedy in his life: his only son Aaron had another rare disease. He aged prematurely, looked like an old man by the time he was a teenager, and died in his teens. Why? I am about to severely criticize the rabbi's reasoning in answer to that question later in this book, but I have nothing but awe at his sufferings and nothing but admiration for his endurance. More importantly for this book, I take his question so seriously that I had to write this book to try to answer it. Here is the rabbi's question:

> I believed that I was following God's ways and doing his work. How could this be happening to my family? If God existed, if he was minimally fair, let alone loving and forgiving, how could he do this to me? And even if I could persuade myself that I deserved this punishment for some sin of neglect or pride that I was not aware of, on what grounds did Aaron have to suffer?

Annie Dillard writes of a burn patient she read about in the newspaper. The case so haunted her that she stuck the clipping up on her mirror. The prognosis was unrelievable, agonizing pain all over the patient's face for the rest of her life. Worse, it happened twice. Just as the effects of the first accident were wearing away, a second came which was far worse, in fact, incurable. It was not her fault. She was a good person. Why do such very bad things happen to good people? God could have arranged the accident for some Mafia chief instead. Why didn't he?

There is a man in Chicago who has loved one woman deeply, truly, and totally all his life. He is a true romantic and a deeply pious Christian. The woman is his wife, or rather was his wife. For one day she dropped on him the most devastating news a man can ever hear: she did not love him and she was leaving him forever.

For years and years after this, he continued to court her. Every day he came to her apartment building and walked around it. She would not let him in. He never gave up. Finally, she gave in, tried coming back to him, then walked out again. He loves her still. That man has suffered so deeply and continually that everyone who knows him says he is the most powerful healer and comforter they ever met. He has healed countless other hurts, but he cannot heal his own. He knows what his suffering is good for, but that does not justify it. Why couldn't God heal all those other people without hurting him so?

Julia was the most loving, friendly, cooperative wife you could imagine. She was also a committed Christian with deep faith and trust in God. Her husband Barry seemed a likeable chap, though with some deep hurts and mix-ups. His parents were divorced, his father used to beat him, and he had learned to distrust the world and God—until he met Julia. Julia was the world to him—a new world. She taught him to trust again, to trust God too. They were deeply in love. Both knew that their marriage would have its problems because of Barry's background, but both were willing to risk it and work at it.

Now, twenty years later, after many ups and downs, Barry has left Julia and has become an alcoholic. Because one summer night a police officer came to their door with the unbelievable news. Their teenaged son, the apple of their eye, who was planning to enter college in the fall, had been killed in an auto accident.

Barry simply collapsed. He refused to talk to Julia, blamed everything on her, and drank himself into oblivion. Julia was left with her teenaged daughter Jill. Jill saw the sufferings her father put her mother through and vowed a war on men for the rest of her life. She became a hard, hating person, hating God above all, the God she had trusted for fifteen years and who had let her down so horribly and unendurably. If God were real, she thought, he would have seen her breaking point and not brought her past it.

As for Julia, her doom was less spectacular but the worst of all. She retreated into a shell of dullness and depression. She never smiled any more. She looked twenty years older. She moved away from family and friends whose attempts to cheer her up and help her she found unendurable. Now she lies in bed at a mental hospital most of the time and stares blankly at nothing—the nothing her life has become. Her only passion is that she hates God.

Julia's case is fictional. But cases like it are factual. If even one case like Julia's exists, it seems to disprove God, a God who supposedly knows and loves and provides for each one of his children. An omnipotent God could have stopped that auto accident and saved four lives, one body and three souls. He didn't. Therefore either he doesn't care, and then he is not all good; or he doesn't know, and then he is not all wise; or he isn't able to, and then he is not all powerful. In any case, the God of Christianity, the God of the Bible, the God millions believe in, is a myth. The facts of life prove that. Don't they?

Here is the most powerful argument for atheism I have ever seen anywhere in the literature or philosophy of the world. Surprisingly, it was written by a great Christian, Dostoyevski. It is Ivan Karamazov's challenge to his believing brother Alyosha, in *The Brothers Karamazov*. Ivan is reciting horror stories of the suffering of innocent children:

This poor child of five was subjected to every possible torture by those cultivated parents. They beat her, thrashed her, kicked her for no reason till her body was one bruise. Then they went to greater refinements of cruelty—shut her up all night in the cold and frost in a privy, and because she didn't ask to be taken up at night (as though a child of five sleeping its angelic, sound sleep could be trained to wake and ask), they smeared her face and filled her mouth with excrement. And it was her mother, her mother did this. And that mother could sleep, hearing the poor child's groans! Can you understand why a little creature who can't even understand what's done to her should beat her little aching heart with her tiny fist in the dark and weep her meek, unresentful tears to dear, kind God to protect her? Do you understand that, friend and brother, you pious and humble novice? Do you understand why this infamy must be and is permitted?

Anticipating and rejecting one of the great traditional answers to the problem of evil, the notion of solidarity in sin (original sin) and in salvation (vicarious atonement), Ivan argues further:

> Listen! If all must suffer to pay for the eternal harmony, what have children to do with it, tell me please? It's beyond all comprehension why they should suffer, and why they should pay for the harmony. Why should they too furnish material to enrich the soil for the harmony of the future? I understand solidarity in sin among men. I understand solidarity in retribution too; but there can be no such solidarity with children. And if it is really true that they must share responsibility for all their fathers' crimes, such a truth is not of this world and is beyond my comprehension.

> And so I hasten to give back my entrance ticket, and if I am an honest man I am bound to give it back as soon as possible. And that I am doing. It's not God that I don't accept, Alyosha, only I most respectfully return the ticket.

> Tell me, yourself, I challenge you—answer. Imagine that you are creating a fabric of human destiny with the object of making men happy in the end, giving them peace and rest at last, but that it was essential and inevitable to torture to death only one tiny creature—that baby beating its breast with its fist, for instance—and to found that edifice on its unavenged tears, would you consent to be the architect on those conditions? Tell me, and tell the truth.

The case against God can be quite simply put like this: How can a mother trust and love a God who let her baby die?

The examples I have mentioned are special. But the strongest case against God comes not from them but from the billions of normal lives that are full of apparently pointless suffering. It is not just that the suffering is not deserved; it is that it seems random and pointless, distributed according to no rhyme or reason but mere chance, and working no good, no end. For every one who becomes a hero and a saint through suffering, there are ten who seem to become dehumanized, depressed, or despairing.

And the universality of it—there's the rub. Your neighbor, your best friend, your doctor, your auto mechanic all have deep and hidden hurts that you don't know about, just as you have some that they don't know about. Everybody out there is hurting. And if you don't know that, you're either very naive and believe in people's facades, or so thick-skinned that you don't hurt yourself and don't feel other people's hurts either.

I don't mean to insult anyone; we all do a lot of cover-ups. It's our animal instinct to cover up our wounds so that they don't get hurt more. Just as animals do this to their bodies' wounds, we do it to our souls' wounds. We are all involved in a universal cover-up.

One part of this wounding that everyone is involved in is the family. Everyone is born into a family, and most people go on to make new families. The family is the first and closest source of the I-Thou relationship. But this source of our deepest loves is also the source of our deepest hurts. If you are part of a family, whether it is a home broken by divorce or alcoholism or resentment, or whether it is unbroken, you know how those closest to you hurt you the most, whether deliberately or not. And if you are not part of a family, you know the even deeper hurt of loneliness.

Look at people on the street. Look at faces. Really look. Especially on a big city street. They're not only busy and rushing—that's not so terrible; Jesus was busy and rushing around much of the time too—but they're hurting. Look at the facial lines, the muscles, the hardness, the tautness, the set of the eyes, the suspicion, the dullness. "The mass of men lead lives of quiet desperation," wrote Thoreau.

People hurt less physically in this century, especially this generation, than ever before, largely due to the progress of medicine. There are anaesthetics, one of the greatest inventions of all time. There are cures for more and more diseases. Industrial society gives most people a comfortable life, a life only the wealthy few used to have. Most people go through seventy or eighty years with less than half a dozen occasions of really agonizing, unendurable physical pain. A hundred years ago you were lucky to get through a single year without pain that we would today call terrible. Think of a world without anaesthetics. Think. When was the last time you felt the equivalent of a sword through your arm?

Yet people are hurting far more psychologically and spiritually today than ever before. Suicides are up. Depression is up. Mindless violence is up. Boredom is up. (In fact, the very word *boredom* does not exist in any premodern language!) Loneliness is up. Drug escapism is up.

But the barbarians are no longer at the gates. The Huns and the Norsemen have long gone. What are we escaping from? Why can't we stand to be alone with ourselves? Solitude, the thing which ancient sages longed for as the greatest gift, is the very thing we give to our most desperate criminals as the greatest punishment we can imagine. Why have we destroyed silence in our lives?

We are escaping from ourselves (or trying to, since yourself is the one thing other than God that you can never escape from) because we all hurt, deep down. Usually it is not an unusual, spectacular, tragic kind of hurt but a general greyness that settles like dust over our lives, a drabness, a dullness, a dreariness, an ugliness, an ordinariness of everything. We go around like robots, obedient to our social programming, never raising the great questions. Our very passions are sleepy. We stumble into bed obedient to sexy advertisements, and out of bed obedient to alarm clocks. We have almost no reason to get out of bed and almost any reason to get in.

This is more tragic, not less, than past sufferings. Deep, passionate sufferings are at least deep and passionate; and if there are very low valleys, there are also very high mountains.

So either you feel great tragedy and ask why, or you don't, and then you are living an even greater tragedy and have even more need to ask why.

Modern man does not have an answer to the question of why. Our society is the first one that simply does not give us any answer to the problem of suffering except a thousand means of avoiding it.

Meanwhile, where is God? He seems part of the problem, not part of the solution. C.S. Lewis found that out when his wife died. He wrote in *A Grief Observed*:

> When you are happy, so happy that you have no sense of needing Him ... you will be—or so it feels—welcomed with open arms. But go to Him when your need is desperate, when all other help is vain, and what do you find? A door slammed in your face.

How easy, how inevitable for the spiritual descendants of Job to look up with the big, betrayed eyes of a hurt child into the face of the Father, now apparently far away, and begin to resent him, or even to hate him.

I will now tell you my most terrible secret.

I get very mad at God sometimes, especially when he lets me get hurt. In fact, I will let a million cats out of the bag. I will tell all the doubters and unbelievers who are reading this a terrible secret most Christians do not tell: I think almost every believing Christian, and probably almost every believing Jew and Moslem too, gets mad at God sometimes. This is a pretty well-kept secret, especially among evangelicals and funda-mentalists. I confess it not to cause scandal or to help the cause of unbelief but simply because it is true, and I believe that we always need truth just as we always need love, because those are two of the attributes of God.

We Christians are pretty ordinary people, subject to the same feelings, failings, and flailings that unbelievers have. One of these is resentment against God when things don't go our way, when life starts kicking us in the pants. We are all little children (there are no grown-ups!), and we all reach a tantrum point when things get bad—some sooner, some later. Sometimes it is passionate anger, sometimes it is dull depression or despair. Psychologists call these the active-aggressive and the passive-aggressive responses. But unless we are puppets, vegetables, or computers, we hit lows in our lives when we simply cannot say to God "I love you" or "Thy will be done" from our hearts.

I will tell you another secret too, because this other secret is also a deep clue to the problem of suffering. This second secret is the subject of a whole book I wrote called *Heaven: The Heart's Deepest Longing*. It is that every single one of us is unhappy on a deep level. Even when our lives are filled, they are empty. Only when we are empty are we full.

I am tempted to explain my paradox, but instead I shall tease you with it and go on to tell you more secrets. One is that our faith is often a largely intellectual thing. We talk a good game of God, but really God makes a pretty unspectacular and non-total difference to our lives most of the time. We don't really practice the presence of God much; we don't really do all to the glory of God. In fact, most of us don't even pray regularly!

Still another secret, less well-kept, is that we have the same moral problems everyone else has, with a better track record only in some areas like drug addiction, murder, and suicide. But there are almost as many gluttons, gossips, adulterers, and misers among us as among anyone else, and as for the two worst sins of all, pride and hypocrisy, we set the world's record.

The Bible, the most honest book in the world, paints a terrible picture of the moral and spiritual failures of God's chosen people, the Jews, throughout their history; and Christians are their successors.

I have in mind not primarily the church's spectacular crimes like witch hunts, the crusades, the Spanish Inquisition, or the Medici popes but the things that keep going on right now in the average Christian home and heart. Chesterton said once that there is only one unanswerable argument against Christianity: Christians. And he showed who he was thinking of first of all when he wrote the following letter to the London *Times*. The *Times* had asked a number of writers for essays on the topic "What's Wrong with the World?" Chesterton's reply is the shortest and most to the point in history:

> Dear Sirs:
> I am.
> Sincerely yours,
> G.K. Chesterton

How does all this confession address the problem of suffering? I am about to say in this book some things that will sound high and exalted and idealistic. I say them for the only reason anyone should ever say anything: because they are true. But when I compare my own life, full of these wide, enormous plains that have yet to feel the footstep of the invading and conquering Lord, with the high mountains of truth that I spy from afar in my dry and dusty flatland, I am impelled by honesty to say what C.S. Lewis said in the preface to his book on the problem, *The Problem of Pain* (which, by the way, is a masterpiece):

> When Mr. Ashley Sampson suggested to me the writing of this book, I asked leave to write it anonymously, since, if I were to say what I really thought about pain, I should be forced to make statements of such apparent fortitude that they would become ridiculous if anyone knew who made

them. Anonymity was rejected as inconsistent with the series; but Mr. Sampson pointed out that I could write a preface explaining that I did not live up to my own principles! This exhilarating programme I am now carrying out.

I write from the common valley, not from any mountain. I have only the ability to write, certainly not the ability to practice. I think most of my readers, who do not preach what I preach, practice what I preach better than I. And we all know which of the two is the more important.

No one after repeated shocks turns easily to God and smiles. Even Job—whose response to his first great load of tragedy was, "The Lord has given and the Lord has taken away. Blessed be the name of the Lord"—even Job only barely endured the second load. God brought him to the brink, to his breaking point. God's brinkmanship is terrifying. Our brink, our breaking point, is usually far sooner than Job's, but God brings us to it just as he brought Job, so that we too, like Job, though with less reason than he, can curse the day of our birth.

Even Teresa of Avila, when thrown off her carriage, slammed rudely to the ground, and deposited in a mud puddle, questioned God. He answered her, "This is how I treat all my friends." Her tart reply was, "Then, Lord, it is not surprising that you have so few." Even saints do not smile sweetly when God throws them into mud puddles. Only pigs do that.

What good to us, then, is a book written on a level of truth and theology and the ideal rather than simply on the level of feeling and psychology and the actual? Here we sit in our mud puddles. Am I about to prattle about trusting God, like Job's three friends? They came to Job on his dung heap with nothing but correct theology. Job could not fault their logic a single time. His only criticism of them was that their words were empty and dead, "words of ashes, maxims of clay." Is that what I offer you?

No. I speak not from the heights but from our shared mud

puddle. But from here we can both see the heights. I have just confessed some of my mud to you so that you would get our relationship right straight off. I address you, dear reader, not as a lecturer addresses an audience but as a friend addresses a friend—in fact, as a starving bum who has found some food addresses his fellow bum. Our only qualification for God's grace is our emptiness, not our fullness; our undeservingness, not our deservingness. "Those who are well have no need of a physician, but those who are sick. I came not to call the righteous but sinners" (Mk 2:17). Similarly, on an infinitely lower level, this book is for empty hearts, not full ones. Read it if you are, like me, hungry.

This book is for everyone who has ever wept and wondered. That includes everyone who has ever been born. For these are the two most distinctively human acts of all. They distinguish us from animals and from computers and from angels.

Do animals weep? I don't know. Perhaps not. Perhaps all animal tears are crocodile tears. But even if animals do weep, they do not wonder. No animal is a philosopher, and wonder is the origin of all philosophy, according to the three greatest philosophers, Socrates, Plato, and Aristotle. When animals suffer, they just suffer. Their song is, "Ours not to reason why, ours but to do and die."

No computer, or artificial intelligence, either weeps or wonders. Computers do not weep because computers do not hurt. They have no feelings, physical or spiritual. And computers do not wonder, do not question, either. They do only what you program them to do. They do not question their programming, unless you program them to do that, and then they do not question *that* programming. We too have been programmed by our heredity and environment, but we question our programming. We doubt. Doubt is glorious. Only one who can doubt can believe, just as only one who can despair can hope, and only one who can hate can love.

No angel, spirit, god, or goddess suffers or questions,

weeps or wonders. Pure spirits do not have bodies with nerve endings all over them, and pure mind never sang, "I wonder as I wander out under the sky." Animals know too little to ask questions and gods know too much.

We alone, we humans, weep and wonder. This book is some wondering about our weeping—wondering why we suffer.

God: How He Comes into It All

I believe in God, the God of the Bible, the all-powerful creator, the all-loving Father. That does not solve my problem of suffering; that makes it worse. Maybe God is going to be part of the solution, but he starts out being part of the problem. For how can an all-powerful and all-loving God allow his innocent babies to suffer? That is the problem; not just suffering but the scandal of suffering in a God-made and God-ruled universe.

This book is not just about suffering but about God and suffering. It is addressed to:
1. orthodox Christians
2. unorthodox Christians
3. non-Christian theists (Jews, Moslems, Unitarians)
4. religious persons in general
5. honest, questioning agnostics
6. rational atheists who disbelieve in God because of the problem of evil
7. rebels, atheists like Camus and Ivan Karamazov who refuse a God who allows such atrocities.

This book is not a neat set of answers for believers to beat unbelievers with. It is a record of a real, honest, personal quest, a lived journey of exploration in life's darkest cave. I do not ask or expect everyone to agree with me at the beginning of the journey, or at the end, only to come along. For this is life's deepest journey, deepest cave, deepest question, for each of the seven people listed above.

Like Job, I have wrestled with God about suffering, as most people have, though I have not experienced unusual suffering, as Job did. This book is the account of the process as well as the results of that wrestling match. I will tell you at the beginning what the results were: I lost. Like Job. And that is the only possible way to win.

Warrant: How Do You Know?

Reader: How dare you try to solve life's darkest mystery?

Author: No, I do not claim to solve it, only to explore it.

Reader: But you clearly have some answers up your sleeve as well as questions. Otherwise you wouldn't have written this book, right?

Author: Right. How clever of you. But I only claim a little light.

Reader: How much?

Author: Enough to live by. Not all the answers. Mystery remains, surrounding all answers and even in all answers.

Reader: But you do have answers?

Author: Yes. Are you suspicious of answers?

Reader: Yes.

Author: But not of questions?

Reader: No. And you?

Author: I love questions too. But what's the point of questions? What do you quest for? Answers! To ask questions but hate answers is like saying you're thirsty but refuse to drink.

Reader: I value an open mind above all.

Author: I value an open mind too. But an open mind is useful just as an open mouth is.

Reader: What do you mean?

Author: For chomping shut on something solid.

Reader: You stole that from Chesterton.

Author: And many other things too.

Reader: Let's get down to brass tacks. What's the proof, the warrant, the foundation for your answers? Where do you get them from?

Author: From five sources. From experience; and from tradition, which is others' experience; and from reason, which is thinking about experience; and from imagination, which I believe is a neglected power of seeing truth; and, finally, from faith.

Reader: Aha! I thought so. I'll bet you believe everything in the Bible, don't you?

Author: Yes, I do. But, like flint against steel, I rub it up against these other four ways of knowing to make some sparks of light come out. And I don't presuppose faith. I don't argue from faith here. The Bible isn't only for believers.

Reader: But you're a believer.

Author: Yes.

Reader: Why should an unbeliever read you?

Author: For the same reason a believer should read an unbeliever. If you know only what *you* know, you don't even know that. You understand things only by contrast. Why should men listen to women? Why should a Republican listen to a Democrat? Why should people who disagree dialog with each other?

Reader: But your subject is well worn. Hundreds of books have been written on it. How is yours different?

Author: I don't know and I don't care.

Reader: What kind of an answer is that?

Author: An honest one. It's not a scholarly book, meant to fill some little technical gap that previous experts have left. It's a book for everyone. The only way I know it's different is that it's mine.

Reader: Shouldn't you at least try to be original?

Author: I don't think so. I think the people who try the hardest to be original end up being silly or else saying old stuff in camouflaged new ways. But if you simply try to tell the truth honestly, as you see it, you usually end up being original without trying. Originality is like happiness: snatch at it and it disappears. The only way to get it is to forget it.

Reader: Are you saying your book isn't original then?

Author: I don't know and I don't care.

Reader: Well, haven't you read the other books on the subject?

Author: Some of them, yes. In fact, I do a lot of piggybacking on them.

Reader: Piggybacking?

Author: The medievals had a saying: "We are dwarfs standing on the shoulders of giants. We see farther than the ancients not because we are taller than they but because we have their shoulders to stand on."

Reader: Such traditionalism! You religious folks are all alike.

Author: No, we're not. And what's wrong with tradition?

Reader: We know much more than the ancients did.

Author: Yes, and they are what we know.

Reader: Hmph! So you use a lot of old books.

Author: Yes. The ones that have stood the test of time and have helped the most people.

Reader: If everybody knows them, why do you repeat them?

Author: Most of them have been forgotten. People used to read classics more. Now, some second-rate philosopher like me has to drag them up again, blow the dust off them, and offer them to the public in a new translation.

Reader: Is that all this book is? A translation of some old philosophers into your own words?

Author: And poets and prophets. And a guy named Jesus. Yes, that's all. It's enough. And it's also the best I can do. I could give you something else, something less than my best. But my father wouldn't like that.

Reader: Your father?

Author: Yes. He taught me to always do my best.

Reader: Where do you find these old books?

Author: In the magic kingdom.

Reader: The magic kingdom?

Author: Yes. It's real. There's a real place you can go where you can really find magic. You can get into other worlds there, like Alice through the looking-glass or the rabbit-hole. Like getting into Narnia through the wardrobe. There are thousands of other worlds there, and holes to get into each one.

Reader: How much does this magic kingdom cost?

Author: It's free.

Reader: Where is it?

Author: In your home town. It's called a library.

Reader: I never thought of books as holes before.

Author: That's because you thought of them only as things, as parts of the world, instead of as doors or windows into other worlds.

Reader: What other worlds? Sounds escapist.

Author: The worlds of other minds. Their authors' minds. That's not escapism because those authors look at this world. What we find there is other doors into this world, other eyes on this world. It's the same world as ours but also a different world because no two people see it in exactly the same way.

Reader: Well, I hope you say some different things about suffering. Because all I've ever heard doesn't satisfy me.

Author: I don't think I'll satisfy you. But I think I'll help you see some things you never saw before, things you never thought of before. Not because I'm so brilliant or original but because you probably didn't read the right books.

Reader: Even if I did, I'd like to see how you use them.

Author: So read on.

Method: How to Cut the Baloney

I hope the reader will enjoy or at least excuse my lapse into dialog. It is a natural mode of speech to most people, more so than monolog. I only wish more writers were like most people. Plato was. Everything he wrote was in dialogs. I have written five books of dialogs and shall write more, God willing. I offer the reader no guarantee that other sections of this one won't fall into dialog by a kind of natural gravity (or levity).

We should say something relatively serious and systematic about method.

1. As you have already seen, I will occasionally write and usually think in dialog, since two minds are better than one. Even God is not only one but three.

2. I will try to combine experience, tradition, reason, imagination, and faith. Why neglect any of our tools?

3. Another point of method is simplicity. Short, simple words, sentences, and sections of chapters. I do not believe that simplicity and profundity are enemies, as many scholars do. All the greatest and profoundest thinkers—such as Jesus, Socrates, Buddha, Solomon, Moses, Mohammed, Lao-Tzu, and Confucius—spoke or wrote in simple language. I want to show the reader that profound things are simple and simple things are profound, by saying profound things simply and simple things profoundly.

4. I look for clues more than answers because I do more looking than calculating. Our brain is divided into two hemispheres, and the right hemisphere with its intuitive, direct, and visionary way of thinking is at least as useful and certainly as profound as the left hemisphere with its rational, calculating way of thinking. Neither one alone is sufficient even for itself; each needs the other, like men and women. But most books, especially in philosophy and especially in modern times, are strong on figuring and weak on seeing. Many philosophers even insist that the first and basic act of the mind is not seeing or understanding but judging, discriminating, distinguishing. But before we can judge that *A* is *B* or discriminate between *A* and *B*, we must know *A* and we must know *B*. How? We *look* with the mind as we look with the eyes.

I do not claim to serve up the total answer to this deep and painful problem but to assemble clues, which are only facets of the answer, like the facets of a diamond. No one can see all the facets of a diamond at once; our angle of vision always limits us. But we can see things of light and beauty. Sometimes we see these in the middle of great darkness, as we find diamonds far underground. We can hope to find light in the darkness of suffering too.

5. Furthermore, the book is personal. I use "I" a lot. We are pilgrims, and we can tell each other travellers' tales as we meet in the noonday heat of our common desert—tales about oases. I am not a preacher or a wise man; I am a thirsty wanderer who has stumbled on some water.

6. The primary place I have found it is where Job found it: in prayer. Everyone in the world wonders about God—who he is, what he is, what his name is. Only one man ever found out God's true name—Moses—because only he was simple-minded enough to ask God (Ex 3)! Job found his answer and found his God at the end of his far deeper quest into the same mystery as mine, but his three friends did not. Why? Because Job asked God! Job prayed. His three friends only philosophized. Job talked *to* God, his three friends only talked *about* God. Even the profoundest philosophy pales next to even the most primitive prayer. St. Augustine's *Confessions* is the greatest masterpiece of religious psychology ever written because it is prayer. He, too, talks to God, not only about him, because he knows God is really present. He philosophizes face-to-face with God. How could the darkness of dishonesty or deceit endure that light? Almost every other sentence of the *Confessions* is a question. Augustine asks God hundreds of questions. That's why he gets hundreds of answers. "Seek and you shall find." Augustine believed that; therefore he sought; therefore he found. Let philosophers today pray, let philosophers shut up and let God show up, and we will soon see a new philosophy to startle the world.

7. Finally, like Augustine, I do not merely skim off the results of my spiritual and intellectual journey, but I give you also the journey itself, the process. Journeys in thought can be

just as real, just as exciting, and just as dramatic as bodily journeys. And they do not deplete your bank account. They even add to your idea account. We should speak naturally of thought-journeys, thought-adventures, thought-explorations. We don't because we think of thinking as something special-ized for intellectuals, or as something abstract and dry and removed from life, or as static and dogmatic and cut and dried. No. Read Socrates or Augustine or Pascal or Kierkegaard, and you will find another kind of thinking. I am not in their league, but I play at their game. This book, in other words, is a quest, not just a question.

In fact, the most valuable things in this book are the things I had no idea I was going to write, the things I learned only by questioning and doubting my old answers. I teach courses in philosophy and religion, and I know most of the arguments and most of the stock answers. Only when I was dissatisfied with these, only when my faith expressed itself in doubting, did I learn new and deeper lessons. The same thing seems to have happened, on an incomparably deeper level, to Job. So this book is more like a diary than a philosophy lecture.

Evil, Suffering, Death, and Sin: Defining Terms

I shall sometimes be talking about the problem of suffering and sometimes, more generally, about the problem of evil. There are three basic kinds of evil: (1) suffering, which is a disharmony or alienation between ourselves as embodied creatures and something in this physical world; (2) death, which is the disharmony, alienation or separation between the soul and the body; and (3) sin, which is the disharmony or alienation between the soul and God.

We shall see connections among these three evils, or alienations, or misrelationships later on. I only want to explain here that I shall sometimes be focusing only on the problem of suffering and at other times be speaking more generally about evil as such. Sometimes it is suffering that is the problem (as in *Job*); sometimes it is evil as such that is the problem (as in philosophers like Augustine and Aquinas who ask, If God is infinitely good, where is there room for any kind of evil?). We want to look at all objections, all aspects of the problem—sometimes specifically suffering, sometimes generically evil.

TWO

Ten Easy Answers

"Humankind cannot bear very much reality."
T.S. Eliot

WE AMERICANS LOVE EASY, fast answers. The devil has sold as many cheap and instant answers as MacDonald's has sold hamburgers. We are impatient with Mystery, especially with a capital *M*. We read a fathomless profundity like the Book of Job and we say, "But what's the bottom line?"

To the deepest mystery of all, the mystery of evil, ten cheap and easy "bottom line" answers are readily available. The one I shall propose instead is impossible to summarize in a bottom line, a statement, or a theory. That is one reason why each of these ten answers is popular, and the eleventh is not.

I will not tell you about the eleventh answer yet because there is nothing more pointless than an answer to a question that is not fully understood, fully posed. We are far too impatient with questions, and therefore far too shallow in appreciating answers. Precisely for the sake of the answer, I linger over the question; precisely to teach appreciation of the answer, I defer it for five more chapters (one on easy answers, one more on the problem itself, and three on clues to a deeper answer). If you get impatient with me during the next five chapters, please read chapter seven before you throw the book away.

Each of these ten answers is a nice, clean shortcut around the mystery. Who wants to steer into the fog bank when there are roads running through the clean air? The Bible looks like a fog bank. Its story centers on mystery. Christianity is not one of the neat, clean little roads. It is like Noah's ark, a big, sloppy, cumbersome old boat manned by a family of eccentrics and full of all kinds of animals who have to be tamed, fed, cleaned, and mopped up after (remember, Noah had no deodorants!); the ten easy answers are like sharp, trim, snappy little craft with outboard motors skipping over the surface of the great deep and leaving the drippy old ark behind as hopelessly inefficient and outmoded. Their only problem is that they don't reach port. They sink. Shiny reason founders; only opaque paradox stays afloat.

To show the truth of this outrageous claim, we must first survey the ten snappy little craft and see why they sink, then more slowly and carefully explore the Christian ark and see why it doesn't.

Two Levels: Thought and Life

One criticism of all ten answers, and I think the most serious one, is that they are not livable. Not only are they irrational, they are inhuman. They do not solve the problem of evil where it hurts, and where it starts, in the guts and in the heart.

The gut-level problem of evil moves us to rebellion rather than to philosophy. It springs from concrete, individual cases of suffering, like dying children—as concrete as a blow to the gut. But the second level of the problem, the thought level, is important too, for it threatens faith, our lifeline to God. The first, personal form of the problem asks, How can I trust a God who lets my child die? The second, philosophical form of the problem asks, Why doesn't the evidence of evil prove that God is not running this show? The personal form feels, the philosophical form thinks. Both are important because both are essential aspects of our humanity.

Few would deny the importance of the first, but some would deny the importance of the second. So a brief word in defense of thought. Thought is important because it is not just subjective, not just a process inside our heads, but it allows us to live in reality, in truth. Thought contacts truth, however fitfully. It opens our inner eyes to the light. God is truth, God is light, God is ultimate reality. Therefore thought is a lifeline to God. That is its ultimate importance.

Outline of the Ten Easy Answers

The problem of evil is created by the apparent inconsistency among four propositions:

   I. God exists
   II. God is all-powerful
   III. God is all-good
   IV. Evil exists

So it seems that we must deny at least one of these four propositions. This is what the ten easy answers do:

   I. Denials of God's reality
      1. Atheism: no God
      2. Demythologism: the fairy tale God
      3. Psychologism: the subjective God
   II. Denials of God's power
      4. Old (polytheistic) Paganism: many Gods
      5. New (scientistic) Paganism: naturalistic God
      6. Dualism: two Gods
   III. Denials of God's goodness
      7. Satanism: the bad God
      8. Pantheism: the blob God
      9. Deism: the snob God
   IV. Denial of evil
      10. Idealism

1. Atheism

There was a rabbi in Auschwitz who kept exhorting his people to believe, to trust God. "God will not abandon us. God will save us." Then came his turn to go to the gas chamber. As he marched in line he kept saying, "God will save us. God will save us." But God did not, and the rabbi's last words, upon entering the gas chamber, were, "There is no God."

But that is not the end of the story, even in Auschwitz. The next man in line, who had constantly heckled the rabbi's faith, entered the same gas chamber with the prayer "Shema Israel" on his lips.

The rabbi seems more reasonable. The simplest, clearest answer to the problem of evil is that there is no God. The reality of evil seems to refute the reality of God, at least the only kind of God most people care about, a God who is both all-powerful and all-good.

There are at least seven reasons why atheism is a cheap answer.

First of all, it is cheap on people. The vast majority of people throughout history believe in a God. However hard evil is to accept, to justify, to explain, or to endure, atheism is even harder for most people. To be an atheist is to be a snob, for it is to assume that nine out of ten people who have lived have lived a lie at the heart of their lives, that the human race has been almost totally suckered in by the biggest con job ever invented.

Second, there may be one very good argument against God—evil—but there are many more good arguments for God. In fact, there are at least fifteen different arguments for God. Evil *is* evidence against God. But most of the evidence is for God. Atheists must answer all fifteen arguments; theists must answer only one.

Third, the very thing that seems to count against God counts against atheism. The very existence of evil proves the existence of God. Here's how. If there is no God, no creator, and no act of creation, then we and our world got here by mere evolution. And if there is no act of creation, then the universe has been in existence always, and there is no first cause. But if the universe has been evolving for an infinite time—and there must have been an infinite time if there is no beginning, no first moment, no act of creation—then the universe should be already perfect by now. There's been plenty of time for evolution to have finished. There should be no evil left. So the very existence of evil and imperfection and suffering in the universe proves the atheist wrong about the universe.

There is another way evil proves God. Moral evil, spiritual evil, proves God. Spiritual evil could not evolve from mindless matter. Moral evil can come only from moral agents, souls. And where did they come from? From something less than themselves, blind matter? Less can't make more; there can't be more in an effect than in its causes. If you admit the existence of moral evil, you must trace it back to moral agents or souls, and souls to God, not to molecules. Our bodies may be made in the image of King Kong, but our souls are made in the image of King God.

Fourth, if there is no God, no infinite goodness, where did we get the idea of evil? Where did we get the standard of goodness by which we judge evil as evil? Worst of all, "if the universe is so bad ... how on earth did human beings ever come to attribute it to the activity of a wise and good Creator?" (as C.S. Lewis argues in *The Problem of Pain*). The very presence of these ideas in our minds, that is, the idea of evil, thus of goodness and of God as the origin and standard of goodness, needs to be accounted for. Big bangs and bumping molecules won't do it.

You can understand the fifth and most important reason why atheism is a cheap answer if you sit by the sickbed of a dying child who demands of you a hope, a meaning, a reason to live and a reason to die. It is a lot easier to live as an atheist than to die as one. The most powerful form of atheism on earth, communism, explains everything but death. Communist philosophers have propagated a party line, an official philosophical interpretation of everything except death. The only thing they say about it is that it is morbid to think about it; it saps your strength away from social progress. But communists too must die. They have no choice. The only choice is to die well or not, and to die well is to die with meaning. Atheism robs death of meaning. And if death has no meaning, how can life ultimately have meaning? For death is the end of life.

Here is a sixth point. I just said it is hard to die as an atheist but relatively easy to live as one. I take that back. Atheism cheapens the world, cheapens us, and cheapens life. To see this, just compare atheist fiction with theistic fiction. Belief in God does not squash man; it raises man to a divine image. Heroism grows only in the sunlight of a divine sun. Squash the ceilings down low and we stoop. In classical Greek drama, in the Bible, in Shakespeare, man is great because he breathes the air of the absolute. In Faulkner, Gide, Sartre, Camus, Beckett and nine out of ten lesser twentieth century writers, man is "full of sound and fury, signifying nothing" because he is a cosmic orphan. His universe is man-sized, not God-sized. Spiritually it is we, not the ancients, who live in a tiny world. Life in that world is a meaningless flicker of a candle for a few years between the cold and barren darkness of two eternal nights. Atheism screws down the manhole covers on the great deeps and flattens the sky to a low ceiling. Instead of a forest of spires and turrets, like the Gothic art that expressed an age of faith, we find ourselves in a ranch-style, flattened, one-story existence.

Seventh, the supreme refutation of the atheist is not present but future, not the idea of death but the lived experience of death. When the atheist meets God face-to-face where he expected to meet nothingness, when the atheist finds that God rather than death is the ultimate reality, he will see that his philosophy was the cheapest answer ever invented—cheap because it refused the only thing that is infinitely not cheap, the God who is infinite value, infinite goodness.

2. Demythologism

Demythologism is atheism for cowards and scholars, people who don't like the sound or reputation of the word *atheist*. Give me a simple, honest atheist any time, one who says straight out that there is no God, there are no miracles, there was no resurrection, it's all a lie, rather than the nuanced scholar who explains that these things are true mythically but not literally; that the concept of miracle is useful when we want to express our wonder at babies or sunsets or a nice man like Jesus; that the idea of a virgin birth is a mythic way of saying that Jesus was a special person; that the resurrection did indeed happen but in the hearts of the disciples rather than in the empty tomb (it was not Jesus but 'Easter faith' that resurrected!).

The demythologizer says he is not an atheist, but his God is not the real, objective creator, lawgiver, miracle worker, and incarnated, risen Savior of the Bible. These things are all supernatural, and the demythologizer identifies the supernatural with the mythic. He does not call these Bible stories false, but he says they are true as fairy tales are true.

The Bible tells two stories about the origin of and solution to evil. The demythologizer does not believe these stories are historically true, i.e., really happened. The first story centers around two trees in a garden, a temptation, and a fall of a couple who tried to be like God. The second story centers around another tree—a cross—another garden, another temptation, and another man, one called the "second Adam." This man claimed to be God, resisted his temptations, died, was buried in another garden, and rose from the dead.

The demythologizer does not believe this literally happened. Three problems remain unsolved if all this is not true: death, morality, and sin. (1) As we lie dying we need more than a fairy tale God and a resurrection of "Easter faith." We need a God who conquered death for us. (2) We need him before that too, e.g., when we want to do something a bit shady and we wonder just how absolute morality really is, whether God or man made it. (Dostoyevski says, "If God does not exist, everything is permissible.") (3) Finally, we need him when we realize that sin is real and that we are unable to save ourselves. We need him to forgive our sin and remove our guilt. Psychologists can cover up the symptoms, the guilt feelings, but only the real God can remove real guilt.

Jesus dealt directly with these three needs. The demythologizer reduces Jesus' real medicine to colored water, to a beautiful fairy tale. Colored water can cure imaginary diseases, but real medicine is needed for real diseases.

3. Psychologism

Another form of wishy-washy atheism, which often overlaps demythologism, is psychologism. Psychologism psychologizes God, subjectivizes God. The God outside of us is rejected, but the terrible term "atheism" is avoided by substituting the God inside of us. "Truth for me" thus replaces Truth; "my God" (or, for the more sociologically inclined, "our God") replaces God. My shoes, my home, my warts, my convictions, my God—all of a piece.

The psychologized God fails in two main areas: honesty and livability. First, the God we make up for ourselves leaves unanswered this most important question: Is this God the one who really exists? Second, the God we make up cannot create us, for we created him. Nor can he save us. He is not stronger than sin or death.

But he is, replies the subjectivist, for he represents the best part of ourselves, which is stronger than sin or death.

This is naive. It is to ignore the nearly unmitigated tragedy that is our history, to deny the reality of human unhappiness and human sin. It is to commit the monstrous *non sequitur* of reasoning from the fact that most of us in twentieth century America are not usually tempted to be cruel to the conclusion that mankind has no problems that mankind cannot solve. The danger of such naivete looms on our horizon in the form of a universal mushroom cloud. The God within shows disturbing tendencies toward deicide.

The hidden and suppressed forces that erupted in the Nazi holocaust are endemic to the race, to the Hitler in ourselves. If there is a God within, there is also a devil within. The real devil is no match for the real God, but the devil within is often a match indeed for the God within.

4. Old Paganism: Polytheism

We now turn from three denials of God's objective reality (easy answers one through three) to three denials of God's power (easy answers four through six). If God is not all-powerful, that explains evil and suffering; it entered the world when God wasn't looking. If God is not creator but Big Brother . . . well, even Big Brother can't solve all your problems.

Paganism is very popular. There must be something to it. Most moderns don't understand what could make a man as clever as Chesterton say, "Paganism was the biggest thing in the world. And Christianity was bigger. And everything since then has been comparatively small."

For one thing, paganism is popular because it has gods. Better have many gods, however weak, however bribable, however silly, than none. "Let Jones worship the sun or the moon, let Jones worship crocodiles, if he finds any in his street, but let not Jones worship the Inner Light. For that means Jones shall worship Jones" (Chesterton again). We must worship something; if not gods above us, then gods within us, i.e., ourselves. And George Macdonald sagely notes that "there is one form of religion in which the more conviction you have the fewer converts you make: the worship of self." Paganism, unlike modernity, is not narcissistic.

For another thing, paganism's many, weak, and bribable

gods seem to account for the manifold, half-good-half-evil, morally imperfect world we see. Many forces in the world; therefore many gods. Goodness weak in the world; therefore goodness weak in the gods. Evil men triumphant? The bad guys got to the divine power buttons before the good guys did.

But the human spirit proved too wise for this apparent wisdom. Paganism did not survive. We cannot believe in the silly shenanigans of Zeus and his cohorts once we begin to ask questions, once we learn to philosophize. Paganism died when philosophy was born. Christianity did not. There have been thousands of intelligent, thoughtful, questioning, honest philosophers who were Christians. There has not been a single philosopher in all of history who defended pagan polytheism literally understood. Pagan philosophy is a contradiction in terms.

Yet paganism does solve the biggest philosophical problem, reconciling God and evil, by weakening "God" to "the gods." Modern forms of paganism do the same thing in a more rational way. We turn to them next.

5. New Paganism: Scientism

Scientism, as distinct from science, is a philosophy. It holds that whatever science cannot detect does not exist. Thus the only God that scientism admits is nature, or the laws of nature, but not anything supernatural. The old pagan way to weaken God and thus solve the problem of evil was to cut him into thousands of little pieces, little gods and goddesses. The new, streamlined, scientific way to weaken God is to flatten him out, to reduce him to nature, or the laws of nature. Spinoza, for instance, defined God as nature looked at from a certain point of view, as whole and one.

Hegel gave this new paganism a big push by reducing God to the end point of a universal process or "dialectic" of historical progress. "Process theology," like Hegel, removes eternity from God and puts him into time. God grows, like us. That's why evil is still around.

Rabbi Kushner fits into this category. His God is not the omnipotent Creator and miracle-worker of the Bible, but some vague, undefined force within nature and subject to nature's laws. His theology is not new. His book was a best seller not because he came up with a bold, new, original answer to the world's oldest problem but because his book was very well written, clear, simple, and direct, and above all because his book was not just theory, just words, but experience; he had lived through the problem with his son. The good rabbi had paid in spades for his philosophy.

The advantage of believing in a naturalistic God is that you can (1) be scientifically fashionable, avoiding the odium of supernaturalism, (2) still have a God of some sort to believe in (a great advantage on sunny days when you don't want to believe all that beauty is nothing but chance), and even (3) preserve God's goodness. You cannot do that with fatalism, which the rabbi mistakenly identifies with traditional religion. Fatalism calls everything the will of God, even Aaron's terrible disease. Fatalism affirms God's power at the expense of God's goodness. Such a God cannot be loved. Kushner's God can. That is an infinite advantage. The fact that millions of Christians and Jews loved Kushner's book probably shows that they were really fatalists and needed Kushner to help them to lose their false faith, their faith in an all-powerful but morally indifferent God. They exchanged that God for Kushner's naturalistic, God; they exchanged power for love.

It is a good exchange, a progress. But perhaps they bought too soon. Perhaps there is a better God on the market, one you can trust (for he has infinite power) as well as love (for he has infinite goodness). Kushner's God fails the crucial test, the death test. A naturalistic God cannot solve the problem of death. Death is nature's trump card. It takes the supernatural to trump death.

6. Dualism: Two Gods

A third way of denying God's power is far less popular than paganism old or new. It is dualism, the belief in two Gods, one good and one evil. This explains the good and the evil in the world. Neither of the two Gods has all the power. That's why goodness doesn't triumph over evil.

There is a whole religion, Zoroastrianism, which is dualistic, but it has relatively few adherents today. Some Christians are in effect dualists when they think of the devil as God's equal and opposite, or adversary, rather than as Scripture portrays him: only a fallen angel and mankind's adversary.

The problem with dualism is that the notion of a wholly evil God falls apart when you push it a little. C.S. Lewis puts it this way: "To be bad, he must exist and have intelligence and will. But existence, intelligence and will are in themselves good. Therefore he must be getting them from the Good Power. . . . Evil is a parasite, not an original thing. The powers which enable evil to carry on are powers given it by goodness." There can be an absolute good but there can't be an absolute evil. Absolute evil is a self-contradiction. Evil is like blindness, good is like sight. Evil is like darkness, good is like light. Evil is like death, good is like life. Evil needs good as a parasite needs its host, as a destructive power needs something good to destroy, but not vice versa. Good does not need evil. Light does not need darkness. God does not need Satan. But Satan needs God.

But though intellectually weak, dualism is psychologically attractive because it results in a dramatic philosophy of life, a warfare between good and evil, which is the theme at the root of all great literature in one way or another. Frankly, I wonder why it is the least popular fake solution instead of the most. Perhaps we fear too much drama.

None of the gods we have looked at so far is wholly trustable, though some of them are good, for none of them is all-powerful either, and to be wholly trustable, a God must be both all-good and all-powerful. For if he is not all-good, he might deliberately do you harm, and if he is not all-powerful, he might accidentally do you harm. Therefore either there is no God who is wholly trustable (a terrifying conclusion, though that fact does not prove it false) or else there is a God who is both all-good and all-powerful.

But if there is such a God, how can he allow evil?

Perhaps he is not all-good. This is the only solution we haven't yet tried.

7. Satanism: the Bad God

An even more dramatic and even more illogical answer to the problem of evil is satanism, the worship of Satan as God. The enthronement of evil answers the problem of evil all right, with a vengeance. Evil is so powerful in this world because Satan is in charge, not God; we ought to jump on his bandwagon, where the power is.

The theoretical problem with satanism is the same as that with dualism. Evil can't be greater than good, because evil is a bent good, a diseased good, a parasite on good. Evil is relative to good. Infinite evil is a contradiction in terms, for infinite evil would leave no room for any good, thus no room for the very existence, intelligence, and willpower of the evil god, angel, or man. And there is the additional problem of accounting for all the goodness in the world if evil is in control. St. Augustine says, "If God is, why is there evil? But if God is not, why is there good?"

The practical problem with satanism is infinitely more serious, and that's putting it mildly. You get what you bargain for. If you join Satan's side, you share Satan's destiny, which is *not* to conquer God (how could a creature conquer its creator? how could finite power conquer infinite power?) but to suffer hell eternally. Hardly a solution to the problem of suffering! Out of the frying pan into the fire.

8. Pantheism: the Blob God

Compared with dualism and satanism, pantheism is a dull, undramatic philosophy, fit for a dull, undramatic age. Externally, ours is an exciting age, but, as observers like Kierkegaard, Nietzsche, Auden, Eliot, Orwell, Riesman, C.S. Lewis, Huxley, and Spengler have noted, internally we are passionless.

I have called the God of pantheism the Blob God. He—or rather it—is simply everything, everything in general and nothing in particular. Everything is a part of it. There is nothing outside it. It did not create a world or persons with free will. It is not a person or a will. For will has preferences and makes distinctions: this and not that. There is no "not that" in pantheism. This accounts for its attractiveness; nothing is forbidden, everything is divine.

Pantheism solves the problem of evil neatly. Evil is part of the blob God too. Hitler is God as well as Christ. God is both good and evil. That accounts for the presence of good and evil in the world, for the world is a part of God, or a manifestation of God. God is "The Force" of the world. And "The Force" has a dark side. That's why the world does too.

Another attractive feature of pantheism is that (as Freud noted) it removes the fear of death. For death is separation of me from the world, and there is no separation in pantheism. We can never fall out of the world, out of everything, out of God. For the pantheist, I am not a really distinct individual face-to-face with God and able to lose my life or my soul. I am part of God, and God can never die.

A third attractive feature of pantheism is that there is no hell. Sin, death, and hell are all dismissed as illusions or failures of insight on our part, partial visions, coming from our lack of enlightenment.

And a fourth attractive feature is that pantheism is esoteric. There is a great snob appeal in saying, "If you were enlightened, if you were one of the few, you would understand."

The problem with pantheism is not that it is unthinkable—great mystics like Buddha and Eckhart and great philosophers like Spinoza, Leibniz and Hegel spontaneously fall into it—but that it is unlivable. You cannot pray to, love, worship, or trust the Blob. According to pantheism, time is an illusion too, for God, the only reality, is perfect and eternal. According to pantheism, the illusion of being somebody is the only thing that has ever happened. Nobodies have been thinking they are somebodies throughout all of non-time. Hm. My refutation of pantheism is not an argument but a yawn.

9. Deism: the Snob God

Pantheism and deism are equal and opposite alternatives to theism. Theism, whether in its orthodox Christian, orthodox Jewish, or orthodox Muslim form, believes that God is both transcendent and immanent, both the infinite creator and present to his finite creation. Pantheism denies God's transcendence, deism denies God's immanence. In deism, God created the world, wound it up like an alarm clock, and left it to tick on its own.

What difference does this theology make to the problem of evil? Pantheism and deism are opposite ways of denying God's goodness, which is one of the ingredients in the problem. Pantheism denies God's all-goodness by saying God is good and evil, for God is everything. Deism denies God's goodness by saying God is neither good nor evil, at least not to us, because God is not "to us" at all. Deism's God does not turn his face to us in love or in hate, in good or in evil. He is indifferent. The God of deism is like Rhett Butler in *Gone with the Wind*: "Frankly, my dear, I just don't give a damn." And we, like Scarlett O'Hara, remain evil, desperately in need of forgiveness and rehabilitation but doomed to loneliness and despair instead.

Thus the greatest argument against deism is not a logical one. Of the fake answers, deism is probably the most logical. It admits the arguments for the existence of God that are based on the evidence in nature. Creation shows a creator, design shows a designer, "the heavens are telling the glory of God." But nature does not tell us whether God is moral (nature is amoral), whether God loves us, or whether he ever came here to save us. We need more than a cosmic clockmaker to save us from sin, emptiness, loneliness, meaninglessness, despair, and death.

Deism attempts to solve the problem of evil by saying that God is in his heaven and that's why all's not right with the world. God is an absentee landlord who lets his tenement become a slum. That explains the filth and crime and suffering in the slum all right, but it doesn't answer the question why the landlord doesn't clean it up if he can. If he's powerful enough to do that (and he must be if he created it in the first place), then it must be a defect in his goodness, in his love and mercy, for him to be such a snob. He may be just—after all, we made the slum, not he—but he certainly is not merciful if he doesn't stoop to help his poor, foolish children. And mercy is at least as important a part of goodness as justice is. The God of deism is not good. He's just *there*. Just there, and not even here.

10. Idealism: the Denial of Evil

If it is illogical to believe all four propositions—(I.) God exists, (II.) God is all-powerful, (III.) God is all-good, and (IV.) evil exists—and if there are terrible problems in denying propositions (I.), (II.), or (III.), then let's try denying that evil exists, proposition (IV.). Let's call this idealism, though that term has many other meanings too. Buddhism, Christian Science, and Theosophy are examples of idealism. Chesterton says somewhere that the great problem of philosophy is why little Tommy loves to torture the cat. Idealism's solution is to deny the cat.

But isn't this patently absurd? It's easy to deny God, or his power, or his goodness, because you can't see God. But you can see evil, can't you? Malcolm Muggeridge says that the dogma of original sin, the most unpopular of all Christian dogmas, is the only one you can prove by the daily newspaper.

Surprisingly, no. You can't see evil, at least not with your physical eyes. David Hume showed that. When you see a murder or a mugging, you see the physical actions which are events, with color, time, kinetic energy, and size. But the evil of the act of murder, like the goodness of the act of love, is not a visible event or thing. What color is evil? What time is goodness? How much kinetic energy does evil have? How many cubic feet does goodness take up?

Hume wrongly concluded from the fact that we don't see goodness or evil with our physical eyes that goodness and evil were mere subjective feelings in the observer, rather than real though invisible qualities of actions and of people's character. But Hume was right in noting that we do not see evil with our outer eyes because evil is not a physical thing. Therefore it is just as possible to deny evil, which is objectively real but invisible, as it is possible to deny God, who is also objectively real but invisible.

It is possible. But it is difficult. For we have an inner eye too, called conscience, and this does see evil. This eye has to be closed or dulled or forgotten, or, more usually, what it sees has to be doubted and reduced to our own feelings. Only then can one say evil is not an objective reality.

The simplest response to idealism is to look at the most obvious and external evil: physical suffering and death. There was once a little boy who was a Christian Scientist. (Christian Scientists are followers of Mary Baker Eddy, who taught that evil was an illusion. They believe that sickness, suffering, and death are illusions which people believe in only because of their lack of true faith or insight.) This little boy went up to his Christian Science preacher and asked him to please pray for his father, who was very sick. The preacher replied, "Boy, you don't understand. Your father only thinks he's sick. Go tell him that. Tell him to have faith." The boy obeyed and met the preacher the next day. The preacher asked, "How's your father, boy?" "Oh, he thinks he's dead."

So much for idealism. We can't honestly deny the cat.

Combined Forms

The most popular answers to the great mystery are usually combinations of answers rather than only one. For instance, "The Force" of *Star Wars,* the *elan vital* or vital force of Creative Evolution, the Oversoul of Ralph Waldo Emerson, the *anima mundi* (soul of the world) of Renaissance alchemists, all combine answer number five (the new paganism, the scientific, naturalistic God) with answer number eight (pantheism, the God who is both good and evil). Theological modernism or liberalism usually combines answer number two (demythologizing) with answer number three (psychologizing). Some combine all four answers just mentioned.

But multiplying zero still gives you zero. If each of the answers has holes, multiplying them only multiplies the holes. If none help, we only multiply helplessness. If none of the foods nourish, then a stew of non-nourishing food will leave us just as starving as any one of its ingredients. If you can't get blood out of a stone, you can't get it out of a quarry either. Our exploration has been a failure.

There is only one thing to do with failure: learn from it, turn your failure into a beginning of success. Back up and start over. Often, the fastest way ahead is to go back.

THREE

Back to the Problem

KNIGHT: I call out to Him in the dark but no one seems to be there.
DEATH: Perhaps no one is there.
KNIGHT: Then life is an outrageous horror. No one can live in the
face of death knowing that all is nothingness.

Ingmar Bergman

WE HAVE MADE TEN JOURNEYS, ten missions, ten experiments.
Every one of them has been a failure. We are back to our
starting point.

Reader: But your starting point is even more of a failure.

Author: How's that again?

Reader: You want to maintain all four propositions: I. God is
real, II. God is all-powerful, III. God is all-good, and IV. Evil is
real. But you can't. There's a logical contradiction there. I
know Christianity and Judaism and Islam all believe those four
propositions. But those three religions have even more of a
difficulty than any of the difficulties you found in the ten
alternatives you just refuted, because the difficulty in those
religions is a logical self-contradiction. But most of the
difficulties you found in the other ten positions were only
practical difficulties. Consider, for instance, Rabbi Kushner's
position. If you deny God's omnipotence, maybe you can't
totally trust him any more, but you can at least avoid logical

self-contradiction, and you can have an intellectually more satisfying answer.

Author: Only practical difficulties, you say? Such lived difficulties as not being able to trust God, if he's weak, or not being able to love him, if he's bad? These are much more serious than any merely logical difficulty. By what right dare you assume that logical difficulties must take precedence over existential difficulties? If we lived by logic, no one would ever fall in love or write music.

Reader: But logic tells the truth; logic is not just a game with concepts. Logic tells you what is. If *A* contradicts *B,* then out there in reality there can't ever be both an *A* and a *B* at the same time. Do you disagree with that?

Author: No.

Reader: Good. Well, then, if there is a contradiction somewhere among your four propositions, then in reality one of them at least must be false.

Author: True. But notice the if. *If* there is a contradiction among my four propositions.

Reader: There certainly seems to be.

Author: But is there, really? Appearance is not identical with reality, to us finite and foolish creatures. We are not infallible. Logic may be infallible, but we are not logic. Haven't you forgotten the first and most important lesson in all of philosophy, the lesson taught to all of us by Socrates, the father of philosophy? That you are wise only when you are humble, that the very first bit of wisdom and the prerequisite for all others is the realization that we are not wise . . .

Reader: You sound as if you want to lecture for a while instead of dialog.

Author: Do you mind?

Reader: Feel free. It's your book.

Author: I love to talk about Socrates. You know, when the Delphic oracle declared him the wisest man in the world, Socrates responded:

What in the world does the god mean? What in the world is his riddle? For I know in my conscience that I am not wise in anything, great or small. Then what in the world does he mean when he says I am wise? Surely he is not lying? For he must not lie.... I was puzzled for a long time to understand what he meant; then I thought of a way to try to find out, something like this: I approached one of those who had the reputation of being wise ... when I examined him, then—I need not tell his name, but it was one of our statesmen—I thought this man seemed to be wise both to many others and especially to himself, but that he was not; and then I tried to show him that he thought he was wise but was not. Because of this he disliked me, and so did many others who were there, but I went away thinking to myself that I was wiser than this man; the fact is that neither of us knows anything beautiful and good, but he thinks he does know when he doesn't, and I don't know and don't think I do; so I am wiser than he is by only this trifle, that what I do not know I don't think I do.

It is not only one of the great passages in the world's literature and the origin of philosophy, of Socratic method, but also an absolutely necessary first lesson for all subsequent philosophy, i.e., wisdom-loving. We are philosophers, lovers of wisdom, not sophists, not wise. *We are not wise.* Pause, let that fact sink in. How readily we rush over it! And then, having quickly admitted it in words, we act as if it were not so, we forget it in practice.

A good example of this forgetfulness is in the Book of Job The clear and powerful point, the blindingly obvious lesson of that book, especially at the end, is the one the author puts into the mouth of God when God finally gives Job his answer, the much longed-for answer to Job's question, which also happens to be our question: Why do the righteous suffer? Why do bad things happen to good people? God's answer is a question:

Who do you think you are, anyway? By what right do you unquestioningly assume that you can know the answer to this question? Are you in a position to answer it? Where were you when I laid the foundations of the earth? Are you the author of this story that is your life? Are you your own creator and designer? By what right does the character claim to have the author's point of view?

But we often miss this obvious answer and look for another. We're more sympathetic to Job's point of view than to God's. We think Job's questions are perfectly good and fair and right questions—they're the questions of this book too, after all. But we forget that questions always presuppose answers to other questions. And Job's question presupposes at least that he can know the answer, that his question is a problem rather than a mystery, a solvable rather than an unsolvable question. His unspoken presupposition is that all questions are solvable, that the idea of any unsolvable question is scandalous and unacceptable.

Readers of the book also often find that scandalous and ignore God's plain reply to Job. Rabbi Kushner, for instance, in *When Bad Things Happen to Good People,* turns the Book of Job on its head to avoid the Socratic wisdom which is its obvious lesson. The rabbi has a clear mind and an excellent style, but his interpretation of Job is one of the most totally wrongheaded interpretations of any book that I have ever seen in print. Job's lesson is that suffering is a mystery, but Kushner insists on rationality. Job teaches humility, Kushner insists on an answer. God himself tells Job he can't know, but Kushner insists on knowing. Job's God asserts his omnipotence; Kushner not only denies his omnipotence but asserts that the Book of Job denies it too. Job makes God the hero and Job the fool; Kushner reverses the roles. Kushner, in fact, makes exactly the same mistake Job made; he puts himself in the right and God in the wrong. Now whether Kushner is right or wrong about God in reality, he is certainly wrong about Job.

He is doing eisagesis, not exegesis. He is reading his own theology into Job, assuming that the author of Job must agree with Kushner. The unconscious assumption works something like this, I think: Job is a great book, and how could a great book possibly disagree with me? Therefore . . .

I do not wish to carp. I believe this unconscious argument actually functions much of the time in all our reading and interpreting. We see others and their writings through our own glasses, our own assumptions, rather than seeing ourselves through theirs. We do not let ourselves be shocked. But we had better. It is training for heaven, where we will all be shocked.

The Jews gave us the Bible. Yet Rabbi Kushner's God is not the God of the Bible but the god of the pagans. Kushner teaches rationalism, naturalism, and self-justification. Like the rest of the Bible, Job teaches mystery, supernaturalism, and sin. If these three notions are unacceptable to the modern mind, well, then the modern mind and the Bible are at odds and one of them must be wrong. Ah, there's the rub, that word "wrong." How dare we call anyone wrong? How can we call ourselves wrong? The Book of Job must say what I say; otherwise, one of us in wrong.

But if nothing is wrong, then nothing is right. And something must be right, therefore something must be wrong. If Scripture is right, the modern mind is wrong. So the modern mind just might be wrong about mystery and supernaturalism and sin.

Reader: Whoa, there. Too fast. How do you know the modern mind is wrong?

Author: I said *may* be wrong. Do you claim for the modern mind what I didn't even claim for Scripture yet—infallibility?

Reader: Don't you believe Scripture is infallible, then?

Author: Yes, I do, but I'm not claiming it yet. But you are claiming it for the modern mind.

Reader: No, I'm not. How?

Author: In practice. By refusing to entertain the possibility that the modern mind might be wrong about mystery and supernaturalism and sin.

Reader: I never refused to entertain that possibility.

Author: Oh. Excuse me. Good. Then let's entertain it. Here it comes. Let's open the door of our mind to it. Let's invite it to come in and sit down and talk with us. Let's listen to it as well as talk to it. That's what it means to entertain a possibility. It's like entertaining a guest. O.K.?

Reader: O.K.

Author: So let's look at mystery. I think we've made some progress in our last chapter when we came back from ten trips empty-handed. We've learned that evil is a mystery rather than a problem.

Reader: What do you mean by that?

Author: Four things. The first is the popular meaning. A problem is solvable, a mystery is not. You can come to the end of a problem, but not of a mystery. Mystery remains mystery, but problem ceases to be problem and becomes solution.

Reader: Then it's hopeless to question a mystery.

Author: No. You can see more light. But you also see more darkness. Like Socrates. You expand your little circle of light that you start out with, but it is always surrounded by more darkness.

Reader: I see. You speak in terms of seeing light rather than solving problems. Is that another difference between problem and mystery?

Author: Yes. That's a second one, a rather technical, philosophical one, but an important one. Mystery concerns seeing, contemplating, intuiting, insight, the first act of the mind in traditional logic. Problems concern solving, by means of reasoning—the third act of the mind. We come to a conclusion and make a judgment.

Reader: What's the third difference?

Author: It explains the first. Gabriel Marcel, who made the distinction between problem and mystery famous, defined a mystery as "a problem that encroaches on its own data," i.e., a question whose object is the questioner, a question we can't be detached from and objective about because we're always personally involved. Falling in love, e.g., is a mystery. Getting to Mars is a problem. Evil is a mystery, not a problem, because we're involved in it. That's why we can't solve it. That's what Augustine found out in the *Confessions* when he said, "I sought, 'Whence is evil?' and sought in an evil way."

Reader: What's your fourth meaning?

Author: The fourth meaning of mystery is the scriptural meaning, which the Church has taken over. A mystery of faith is a truth we couldn't possibly come to know by our own reason and experience but which God has revealed to us. The Trinity, e.g., or God's providential plan to save the whole world through Christ. That's the mystery Paul is talking about in his letter to the Ephesians.

Reader: That sounds positive. I thought mystery was negative, darkness.

Author: Exactly—that's what modernity doesn't understand about it. That's why it's so prejudiced against mystery. There are two different meanings of the word, and they're not only different, they're opposites. The negative meaning is the one you find in the atheistic existentialists: the lack of ultimate meaning, ultimate purpose, the emptiness at the heart of things, the heart of darkness. The ancient Greek version of this was *moira,* blind and irrational fate, which ruled gods as well as men. The ancient Greeks were really the first existentialists, you know. Then their philosophers put light in the place of darkness. Our new existentialists take away that light and revert to the primal darkness of fatalism.

The other, positive meaning of mystery is the one in Job. God has his reasons—good ones—for letting bad things happen to good people. But he's not telling Job, and Job can't find out. Here, darkness is subjective but not objective. Here, our minds are in the dark but God is light. In the other kind of mystery, the existentialists' kind, reality itself is dark and our minds are the standard that judges reality as deficient, as missing what we demand, that is, humanly satisfying explanations. In existentialist mystery, we are light and reality is darkness. In scriptural mystery, reality is light and we are in the dark. In fact, we are dark precisely because reality is light, too light. As Augustine and Aquinas love to repeat, we are like bats or owls; we see shadows well, but not the sun. By its very excess of light the sun blinds us.

Reader: And the sun stands here for God?

Author: Yes, and his purposes. Positive mystery, light appearing as darkness. It's a possibility, isn't it?

Reader: Yes . . .

Author: So just in case it should be true, let's try it, as a thought experiment. Let's back up and look at it. There was no logical answer to our question, remember. All ten paths failed. So let's try a different method, a different approach, not just a different doctrine.

Reader: What approach?

Author: Let's go slower. Let's look instead of reasoning so fast. Let's look at clues instead of demanding total answers right off. Let's amass evidence like a detective looking for clues of God in nature. No one of the cosmological arguments is complete or unanswerable, but the converging clues, the evidence for a divine designer in so many areas of the cosmos, add up to a much stronger picture. Maybe we can do the same in human life for the problem of evil as we can do in nature for the problem of God.

Reader: Are you saying that maybe there is no logical solution?

Author: I'm saying that logical thinking is not the only method, the only string to our bow. I admit that if we ever find a solution, it can't be illogical, it can't be a simple contradiction, because that would be meaningless and unthinkable. For instance, no one can believe that God is both omnipotent and not omnipotent. No one can think that because it just doesn't mean anything. But although our answer, if we ever find one, can't be illogical, I don't think we will arrive at it by logic.

Reader: But if and when we find it, it will appear logical, won't it?

Author: If it's true, it can't be illogical. It may appear to us as supralogical, but not sublogical.

Reader: Why insist on these distinctions? Why hold onto logic? Why not just abandon it altogether, like the existentialists?

Author: Even the existentialists can't abandon it altogether, and most of them know that. We're immersed in logic as we are immersed in air, or language, or grammar. It's the inherent structure of thinking.

Reader: But not of reality?

Author: Yes, of reality too, unless thinking doesn't reflect reality. And then what good would it be? Why think if we can't find the truth, can't find reality? I have better things to do than play with concepts. I don't want to play poker for chips that have value only inside the game. I want to win real money. I want to play with the poker chips of concepts only to win the real money of truth, knowledge of objective reality.

Reader: So you believe objective reality has a logical structure?

Author: Yes.

Reader: Evil too?

Author: I believe objective reality is like light. Light, or meaning, is bigger than logic, just as language is bigger than grammar. But it's not less. The issue is not logic first of all. Logic is only a tool. The issue is meaning.

Reader: Issue? What issue?

Author: The issue between the existentialists and me. About mystery. Once you see that there is mystery, that there's no neat fit between our minds and reality, that there's darkness as well as light (for instance, the mystery of evil), then there are only two alternatives left. Once you leave rationalism, you go either to supra-rationalism or to sub-rationalism, either to Mystery with a capital *M* or to mystery with a small *m,* either to greater meaning or to greater meaninglessness.

Reader: And how does this impinge on our problem, especially suffering? That's what I'm interested in, not all this talk
about logic.

Author: Good. Me too. But we had to take another look at
logic and method and reason and mystery, because it makes a
fundamental difference to everything we'll do from now on,
outside this book as well as in it, in life as well as in thought.

Reader: How?

Author: How you approach the problem of suffering depends
on how you approach life itself. There are only two ways.
Either meaning is surrounded by matter, or matter is surrounded by meaning. Either we and our lives and our
meanings and therefore also our sufferings and whatever
meanings they may have are ultimately only a part of,
surrounded by, and conditioned by the visible immensities of
this material universe, and we find our little meanings in our
little corners of this little world; or else our little minds in our
little corners, and everything else as well—minds and bodies
and our whole universe with every event and every atom that
ever was—is part of meaning, part of something mental, part
of a cosmic plot. Either our lives are a little stage surrounded
by darkness, or else all the world's a stage, and the spots of
darkness are in the plot. Thornton Wilder puts it this way, at
the beginning of his little classic novel about divine providence, *The Bridge of San Luis Rey*: "Some say that to the gods
we are like flies that boys idly swat on a summer day. Others say
that not a feather from a sparrow falls to the ground without
the will of the Heavenly Father." Those are the only two
options.

Make the issue simple and concrete. Look at anything. I'm
looking now at a late spring snowstorm. A surprise, a gift. Is
there a giver? Is it part of anybody's plan? Is it—ultimately,
finally, in the long run—really meaningful, a part of the plot of
our life's story, part of a gift or a task or a work? Is anybody
there? Is the whole world, including every snowstorm and

every star and every headache and every bug and every death and every cancer—is it all between God the storyteller and ourselves, so that this material universe is only the stage setting of the story? Or is the universe a meaningless darkness in which we desperately erect little artificial theaters, light them up with little artificial lights (our reasons), and put on little artificial plays (our lives), whose sole meanings are assigned by their sole authors (ourselves)? The really ultimate question, much more important than the scientific question, is: Who's there? That's why myth is more important than science. Myth is an answer, though an unsatifactory one, to the deeper question, Who's there? Science only answers the question, How does it work? Or at the most, What's there? Science asks what and how, philosophy asks why, myth and religion ask who. Who's in charge here? Who's the author? That's what we really long to know.

FOUR

Seven Clues from the Philosophers

"Philosophy is a rehearsal for dying."
Socrates

WE HAVE AGREED TO LOOK for clues rather than answers, at least for a while, for two reasons. First, because when we look for answers we find only bad ones. Second, because the true answer might be so mysterious and deep that we couldn't get it all at once. It might be like a story. (Tell me the whole story of David Copperfield all at once, or at least in twenty-five words or less, please.) It might be like a person. Reduce a person to a category, to a stereotype. It can't be done. If the answer is like a story or like a person, that would be a richness, not a defect. We would then be glad it is a mystery rather than a problem.

I offer you these clues, arranged in chronological, historical order, because they are the ones I have found, tested, and used. I believe they are true—I wouldn't feed your mind poison— but they are not adequate, not enough. There are two reasons for that. First, no one answer and no one philosopher is enough; to a question as deep as this one, we need an answer so deep that it is multiple, like the eye of a fly. Second, these first seven clues come only from philosophers. Philosophers are important—I am one, after all, and I wouldn't spend my life at something I thought trivial—but they are abstract. The truth has an abstract aspect, but truth is more than something abstract. Ultimately, truth is not a concept but a reality; the true is the real. This is why truth is relevant and practical. It is a road map to real land; it is about our existence, our lives. Good philosophers remember this.

Clue One: Socrates—Intellectual Humility

We have seen this point already, but we have probably also forgotten it already. So it bears repetition.

Socrates' point is that there are only two kinds of people in this world: the wise, who know they are fools, and fools, who think they are wise.

Wisdom, in the realm of the mind, is exactly parallel to sanctity, in the realm of the heart or will or spirit. Just as the wisest philosophers, like Socrates, admit they are fools, so the greatest saints admit they are sinners. Thus there are again only two kinds of people: saints, who say they are sinners, and sinners, who think they are saints.

Just as spiritual humility is lesson one in sanctity, so intellectual humility is lesson one in philosophy. Asked what were the four cardinal virtues, St. Bernard replied, "Humility, humility, humility, and humility."

We have already seen, in our last chapter, how Socrates' humility solved the riddle of the oracle. It was a lesson he never forgot and always tried to teach as the first step of his Socratic method. Only when we know that we don't know, do we sincerely question and inquire.

Questioning is equally far removed from both dogmatism (thinking you have all the answers) and skepticism (believing there are no answers). Neither the dogmatist nor the skeptic questions. Dogmatism is intellectual pride and skepticism is intellectual despair; they are equal and opposite extremes, like pride and despair in the moral sphere. Questioning, therefore, is opposed to pride. No one should ever discourage ques-

tioning, whether in themselves or in another. Jesus always
respected his disciples' questions, no matter how foolish they
were. Parents, teachers, or preachers who discourage questioning are acting like dogmatists or skeptics; they are either
arrogant or cowardly, prideful or despairing.

I put lesson one first not only because it is historically first,
with Socrates, the father of philosophy, but more importantly
because everything else in this book must be colored by the
lesson. Job's three friends made the mistake of forgetting it,
and this invalidated everything they said, however correct it
was. They thought they knew it all, therefore even when they
did, they didn't.

Unfortunately, religious people have a tendency to be more
like Job's three friends than like Job. That's why you don't want
to buy what they're selling. But Job learned lesson one; in fact,
Socrates' lesson one is the major lesson of the book of *Job*.
That's why Job and Socrates are deep brothers under the skin.

To see the Socratic wisdom of Job more explicitly, we must
see that Job's question is implicitly: *Is my suffering worth it?* To
answer that question we have to know the end of the story, the
point and purpose of it all. And only the author of the story
knows that, the reason for creation, the meaning of man. And
that is precisely the point of *Job*. It is foreshadowed in the great
twenty-eighth chapter, on the search for wisdom:

"Man puts his hand to the flinty rock,
and overturns mountains by the roots.
He cuts out channels in the rocks,
and his eye sees every precious thing.
He binds up the streams so that they do not trickle,
and the thing that is hid he brings forth to light.

"But where shall wisdom be found?
And where is the place of understanding?
Man does not know the way to it,
and it is not found in the land of the living." (Jb 28: 9-13)

"God understands the way to it,
and he knows its place.
For he looks to the ends of the earth,
and sees everything under the heavens.
When he gave to the wind its weight,
and meted out the waters by measure;
when he made a decree for the rain,
and a way for the lightning of the thunder;
then he saw it and declared it;
he established it, and searched it out.
And he said to man,
'Behold, the fear of the Lord, that is wisdom;
and to depart from evil is understanding.'" (Jb 28: 23-28)

Clue Two: Plato—No Evil Can Happen to a Good Man.

Plato is to Socrates what St. Paul is to Christ, or even what the creeds are to Christ. Plato systematized Socrates. Plato grew the seeds that Socrates planted.

Ralph Waldo Emerson says that "Plato is philosophy and philosophy Plato." Alfred North Whitehead calls the whole history of Western philosophy "footnotes to Plato." In Plato's thirty dialogs you can find just about all the major questions and nearly all the major answers of the next 2400 years of Western philosophy.

Suppose we were to ask Plato this question: Of all your many ideas, what is the greatest, the profoundest idea that you have ever had? What's the big idea, Plato? What would he say?

(That is a good question to ask a thinker. Karl Barth, perhaps the greatest theologian of the twentieth century, was asked that question once. His answer was, "Jesus loves me.")

Plato would answer, "The idea of the Good. That's the big idea." The Good is the absolute, the ultimate reality. Ultimate reality is both fact and value. It is not a brute fact but goodness, value. Goodness is not just an abstract idea to be contrasted with the real world. The ideal is real. Goodness is real. Values are not just human, not just in our heads, not just subjective.

What then is evil? And whence does it come? Plato has no clear answer to that question, and he does not pretend to. (He has learned lesson one.) But he does give us some good clues. One of them is the following:

Reality has laws. They are not man-made laws, norms (*nomoi*), which can be disobeyed. They are natural laws, laws of nature, truths (*logoi*), which can never be disobeyed. They are like the laws of mathematics: two plus two will never be three no matter what we do. Triangles will never have four sides.

Here is one of the laws of ultimate reality, or the Good. It sounds outrageous. Yet it is the central conviction of Socrates' life and death as summarized in his great swan song, the *Apology*. It is the one thing he says he is unqualifiedly certain of. Plato's greatest work, the *Republic,* tries to prove it is true; in fact, this is the central theme of the *Republic*. All the political details are there only to illustrate or prove this fundamental point.

This is the point, the paradox, the clue: "The eternal law (logos) forbids a good man ever to be harmed by a worse, in this life or in the next." The *Republic*'s version of the same principle is that "justice (goodness) is always more profitable than injustice."

Reader: But . . . but . . .

Author: See the spirit of Socrates has triumphed again; we revert to the dialog form once more. Good. Out with your doubt. But what?

Reader: But it happens all the time. Bad things happen to good people. Nice guys finish last. The Red Sox haven't won a world championship since 1918. Charlie Brown can't fly a kite or kick Lucy's football. Bad guys kick good guys around.

Author: And so it follows from this that bad guys are happier, hurt less, profit more? That injustice is more profitable than justice?

Reader: Well, I don't want to simply say that.

Author: Yes, you do. Unless you agree with Plato.

Reader: I want to agree with Plato, but the world just isn't like that. How could he be so unrealistic?

Author: Read the *Republic* and see.

Reader: Could you summarize it for me?

Author: I could, but I won't, unless you promise to read it. Otherwise my summary would be stealing from you the opportunity to read one of the greatest books ever written. No one should be allowed to die without reading Plato.

Reader: I promise to read him. Now tell me.

Author: The riddle of how Plato could possibly believe what seems so contrary to experience, that bad things never do happen to good people, is solved by another riddle, the one Socrates received from the oracle, spent his whole life looking into, and revolutionized Greek thought with when he got its answer. The second riddle is "know thyself," and the answer is that I am essentially not this visible hunk of stuff, but a soul, a spirit, an I, a self, a personality, a character.

Reader: How does that solve the first riddle?

Author: When I harm your body, I do not harm your soul but my own soul. Each of us, simply by having a soul, has the perfect defensive weapon, a mirror that can reflect back all harm upon the aggressor. The only person who can do my real self harm is me. You can only harm my body, this old house. You can burn down my house, but you can't get me.

Reader: That's silly. If I harm your body, I harm your soul too. I make you bitter and angry.

Author: Not if I don't let you. You *tempt* me to bitterness, but I don't have to succumb. Ultimately the choice is up to me, if I am a normal, free adult. You can make it much harder for me to be good, but you can never make it impossible. Bad things can just happen to my body but not to my soul.

Reader: So the answer to why bad things happen to good people is simply that they never do!

Author: Yes, because "people" means not bundles of molecules. That's what lies in a grave when the soul isn't there any more and walks around when the soul is there. The soul is me.

Reader: Isn't this a bit one-sided, ignoring the body so?
Author: Yes, I think it is. But isn't that a minor correction? Isn't Plato basically right? Am I not essentially soul, character, personality? And isn't that impervious to harm from things like swords or hemlock or prison?
Reader: Well, yes, but . . .
Author: O.K., then. I have some buts to add too. Yet the point is made. It's not a complete answer, but it's something. A clue.
Reader: I hope you also consult some less idealistic and more commonsensical philosophers.
Author: I will. The next one is Aristotle, the master of common sense.

Clue Three: Aristotle—Happiness Is Not a Warm Puppy.

The most popular book of the master of common sense is his *Ethics.* This book, like most premodern books on ethics, asks three basic questions where modern books on ethics ask only one or at the most two. C.S. Lewis likens these three questions to the three questions which the sailing orders of a fleet of ships need to answer. First, they need to know how to cooperate, how to avoid bumping into each other. This is like the ethical question of how we should treat our neighbors, or social ethics. It is the only question most modern ethics deals with. Second, the ships need to know how to stay shipshape, how each one can avoid sinking. This is like the question of individual virtues and vices, the question of character. Ancient ethics dealt even more with this question than with the first question. But most modern books on ethics ignore it altogether, as in, for instance, so-called "values clarification," which is to real ethics what pop psychology is to real psychology. But the third and most important question of all for Aristotle and the ancients is the question of the *summum bonum,* the greatest good, the highest value, the ultimate end, point, and purpose of human life. This is like the sailing order telling the ships why they are at sea in the first place, what their

mission is. Modern people don't normally think of this
question as an ethical question at all. But it's the most
important question in ethics.

Aristotle's answer to this question is happiness. Happiness
is the end of life. For everyone always pursues, desires, and
seeks everything else for this reason, for happiness. But no one
seeks happiness for any other end. No one asks, "What good is
happiness? It can't buy money." As Pascal says:

> All men seek happiness. There are no exceptions. However
> different the means they may employ, they all strive towards
> this goal. The reason some go to war and some do not is the
> same desire in both, but interpreted in two different ways.

But the meaning of the word *happiness* has changed since
Aristotle's time. We usually mean by it today something
wholly subjective, a feeling. If you feel happy, you are happy.
But Aristotle, and nearly all premodern writers, meant that
happiness was an objective state first of all, not merely a
subjective feeling. The Greek word for happiness, *eudaimonia,*
literally means good spirit, or good soul. To be happy is to be
good. By this definition, Job on his dung heap is happy.
Socrates unjustly condemned to die is happy. Hitler exulting
over the conquest of France is not happy. Happiness is not a
warm puppy. Happiness is goodness.

At issue here is more than the use of a word. At issue is the
most important question in the world. What is the greatest
good? What gives our lives meaning? What is our end?
Modernity answers, feeling good. The ancients answer, being
good. Feeling good is not compatible with suffering; being
good is. Therefore the fact of suffering threatens modernity
much more than it threatened the ancients.

Furthermore, the most popular modern answer to the
question of what it means to be a good person is to be kind. Do
not make other people suffer. If it doesn't hurt anyone, it's

O.K. By this standard, God is not good if he lets us suffer. But by ancient standards, God might be good even though he lets us suffer, if he does it for the sake of the greater end of happiness, perfection of life and character and soul, that is, self.

Notice how Aristotle's point piggybacks on Socrates' point. Aristotle adds the body as a real though secondary ingredient in happiness, as Plato did not; he says complete happiness includes sufficient bodily goods because he defines a person as soul and body, not just soul. But Aristotle admits that the soul is primary; in fact, he calls it my form, that which makes me me. It's my me-ness, my essence.

So suffering does not refute belief in a good God to the ancient mind because a good God might well sacrifice our subjective happiness for our objective happiness. But the modern mind finds it hard to make that distinction (between subjective happiness and objective happiness); therefore, it finds it hard to believe in a good God who lets us suffer.

A quick reflection on human parenting tells us that we know deep down that the ancient mind is right. Parents who want only freedom from suffering for their children are not wise parents. What parent says, "I don't care what you do, just enjoy yourself"? Grandparents say, "Run along and play," but parents add, "But don't do this or that, and be sure to do so and so."

Nowhere in the Bible is God ever described as our grandfather. But the man who definitively showed us God, like a transparent window, consistently called God "Father."

Clue Four: Boethius—All Fortune Is Good Fortune.

Of all the books of philosophy ever written, no one comes closer to a purely rational solution to the problem of suffering and how to reconcile it with belief in God than *The Consolation of Philosophy* by Boethius. It is seldom taught; yet I have had ccess with this book in class than any other (with the possible exception of Augustine's *Confessions*). Students are more fascinated with its argument, appreciate it more, and learn more valuable lessons from it, by their own admission, than from any other book in the history of philosophy.

There are so many clues to our mystery in this book that I could write a whole book, a rather long one, commenting on this short book of Boethius. I select here only one clue, the outrageous claim that all fortune is good. It is similar to Socrates' point that no evil can ever happen to a good man, but it is proved in a different way. Boethius tries to prove it by natural reason alone, as Socrates did; but what he proves is one of the most incredible claims in Scripture, "All things work together for good to those who love God" (Rom 8:28).

There are two different ways Boethius proves this conclusion: from experience and from principles. The argument from experience is that bad fortune is really just as good for you as good fortune is, in fact, it is better, because, he says, bad fortune teaches, while good fortune deceives. When the worldly toys in which we foolishly place our hopes for happiness are taken away from us, our foolishness is also taken away, and this brings us closer to true happiness, which is not in worldly things but in wisdom. Bad fortune wakes us from our deceptive dream, and thus is good for us—assuming, as the courageous and honest ancient mind nearly always assumed, that we need truth more than comfort, that we need not false happiness but true happiness.

The other way Boethius proves that all fortune is good is by deduction from the principle of divine providence. The skeptic's argument is thus stood on its head. For the skeptic argues from the assumption that all suffering is bad to the conclusion that there can be no all-good and all-powerful God providentially in charge of this world. Boethius argues from the assumption that there is such a God to the conclusion that not all suffering is bad. If God is in fact all-good and all-powerful, Romans 8:28 logically follows.

Whose assumption is more certain? Is the skeptic sure that all suffering is bad? Has he never learned from suffering?

Clue Five: Freud—The Life-Wish vs. the Death-Wish

But is Boethius and the ancient mind right in being so tough, in preferring truth to contentment, objective happiness to subjective happiness, wisdom of mind to peace of mind, being good to feeling good? Doesn't the modern mind, typified by Freud, say the opposite?

No, not even Freud. Toward the end of his life, he too turned a bit heroic when he discovered *thanatos*, the death-wish. We all have two primordial, unconscious drives, according to Freud: *eros*, the life-wish, and *thanatos*, the death-wish. Both flow from the pleasure principle, our innate drive for pleasure and against pain. *Eros* drives us forward to life, birth, growth, sex, reproduction, creativity, challenge, and future, even at the price of suffering. Both love and work, both childbirth and art, demand suffering. One of Beethoven's biographers listed the three greatest and hardest human tasks as heroism, childbirth, and creative work. For Freud, heroism *is* childbirth and creative work, and he says the two things everyone needs most are love and work. Both involve suffering. In fact, the same kind of suffering: birth pangs.

The other half of the pleasure principle is *thanatos*, the death-wish. It drives us not forward but backward, back to the only time and place where we ever had what we want—total pleasure and no pain—back to the womb. This, according to Freud, helps account for aggression; we resent life for birthing us into pain and we take our vengeance on life by destruction. Each individual and civilization makes a fundamental choice between these two innate options. Heroism is the affirmation of *eros* and the refusal of *thanatos*. Toward the end of his life, Freud worried about the choice our Western civilization was making as he saw Hitler, the incarnation of the death-wish, coming to power.

Without meaning to do so, this old atheist Freud has provided us with a tool for the defense of theism. Suffering is not the worst evil if it is in the service of *eros*. It is admirable to prefer the reality principle to the pleasure principle, even if it makes us unhappy. Freud himself rejected God for a psychologically admirable reason; he thought God was a comfortable myth, an invention of man to shield him from unhappiness.

Thus Freud comes back to Aristotle and Boethius in the end: we need truth, even if we must suffer for it, more than we need comfort or pleasure. We need to hit our head on a low-hanging tree branch after coming out of our study with our head full of subjective fantasies so that we can thank the branch for slapping us back to the thing we need most: reality. We need to avoid the "descent into hell" that Charles Williams describes in the absolutely terrifying psychological novel by that title: the descent into the self, the withdrawal from reality and even from concern for reality. It is a hell which Williams succeeds in making far more terrifying and far more convincing than Dante's torture chambers, contrived and external as they were. We need to be exiled from Eden and prevented by the severe mercy of death and the seraphim's flaming sword from returning to Eden. We need the wilderness of suffering and death. Returning to Eden would be spiritual death for us.

A God who does this to us is not a bad God.

A question that remains unanswered by philosophy and by natural reason is, Why do we need such hard lessons? What's wrong with us, that we need pain and death? It is fools who learn by experience, they say; why are we fools?

The Bible answers this question by the story of the fall of man. But we are not that far along yet in our exploration. Perhaps reason and experience define only the strangely shaped hole in us, like a lock, and something more than reason and experience supplies the equally and similarly strangely shaped key.

Clue Six: Marcel—Hope

The existentialist philosopher (he prefers "personalist" or even "Socratic") Gabriel Marcel defines hope more mysteriously and more cosmically than we usually do:

> Hope consists in asserting that there is at the heart of being, beyond all data, beyond all inventories and all calculations, a mysterious principle which is in connivance with me, which cannot but will that which I will if what I will deserves to be willed and is in fact willed by the whole of my being.... The simplest illustrations will be the best. To hope against all hope that a person whom I love will recover from a disease which is said to be incurable is to say: It is impossible that I should be alone in willing this cure; it is impossible that reality in its inward depth should be hostile or so much as indifferent to what I assert is in itself a good.

Your best friend is dying. You say, this cannot be! This is denial. But is it wholly false? Your friend does die. Therefore your denial of death was false, wasn't it? Yes, if the only thing it said is that he will not die. But perhaps you were denying something else, perhaps you were denying that this was the whole truth, the whole story, the deepest and final thing. Perhaps your denial unconsciously saw the deep truth that there are things stronger than death, such as life, love, and meaning.

The same with suffering. Are the appearances the whole story? Hope says not. The appearances are only the facade, the epidermis, the surface. Below the surf-face lie the deeper tides.

Is there any evidence that this prophetic word of hope is true and not mere desperate wishful thinking? Yes: the consequence of denying it. This alternative vision of life is ultimate despair instead of ultimate hope. When Bertrand Russell was asked what he expected to find at death he replied that there was always darkness within, and now there will be also darkness without, forever. Ecclesiastes called life "vanity of vanities" because death had the last word. Sartre called it simply "absurd." Macbeth called it "full of sound and fury, signifying nothing." This is the vision of life that has inspired most modern novels and most modern life. A life without hope simply cannot survive for long, whether in an individual or in a civilization; and when it expires, it will go, as T.S. Eliot said, "not with a bang but a whimper."

The alternative vision says that beyond death and beyond suffering there is life and joy. The point of everything, and therefore the point of suffering, too, is life and joy. We are bits of darkness surrounded by a great light, not bits of artificial light surrounded by cosmic darkness. We are shadows destined to disappear in an eternal light when our substance is revealed, not flickering candles doomed to fitfully sputter and expire in the darkness.

Suffering is therefore birth pangs. Beyond suffering there is the joy of new birth. That is the word of hope. I have not proved its vision true. But no one has ever proved it false either. We are perfectly free to hope, to choose life.

Clue Seven: C.S. Lewis—The Principle of First and Second Things

Lewis was something of a philosopher as well as a novelist, theologian, and essayist. Prepared to teach philosophy, he taught literature instead only because there was no position open in philosophy at Oxford at the time. The fact that his philosophy is intelligible to the general public, like Socrates', should not prejudice us against him, as it prejudices the establishment. Here is one of the many ideas Lewis culled from the giants ("we are dwarfs standing on the shoulders of giants") and formulated more clearly than they did. He calls it, in an essay by that title, the principle of first and second things.

It could be formulated this way: things have different values, some greater than others. Whenever we reverse this real hierarchy of values and treat a lesser value as though it was greater value, whenever we sacrifice a first thing for a second thing, we not only lose the first thing but the second thing as well. For instance, when we treat a hobby or a pet as more important than a person, we not only sacrifice persons but we also spoil our enjoyment of the hobby or the pet, making it an addiction, an obsession. When we become hypochondriacs and treat bodily health as more important than anything else, we worry ourselves sick. When a nation treats its own survival as its highest goal rather than any purpose or value for which to survive, it will not survive for long.

Values are related to each other like a chain of rings. Lesser values are not independent of greater ones. This is why the attempt to put second things first never can work. Values are as objective as mathematics. It never works to count a smaller number as more than a greater number, no matter how sincere you are and no matter how cleverly you try. Similarly, it never works to treat really second things first and really first things second, any more than it works to walk on your head or grow a tree with its roots in the air.

Now how does this principle apply to the problem of suffering? Let us suppose, as common sense asserts, that we are creatures of both body and soul, with soul the more important of the two. Nearly everyone agrees with this principle in practice; for if you had to choose between paralysis of body or of mind, between being a physical or a mental cripple for the rest of your life, nearly everyone would choose the former. To lose your mind is to lose yourself.

Now if soul is greater in value than body, then the good of the soul is greater than the good of the body and the evil of the soul is greater than the evil of the body. What is the good of the body? Health, pleasure, freedom from suffering. What is the good of the soul? Wisdom and virtue.

If we need to suffer to become wise, if we need to sacrifice some pleasure to be virtuous, if too much pleasure would make us fools, if an easy life would make us less virtuous—if this were so, then suffering would not contradict a good God. God might use suffering to train us, sacrificing the lesser good for the greater. The principle of first and second things is another way of seeing or saying the thing we have already seen in two or three other ways. The clues converge.

A special way in which the physical evil of suffering leads to a spiritual good is through solidarity in suffering. When people suffer together they band together. Families were never so close and loving as in the Great Depression of the thirties. Every family or group of friends can say with warmth, "Remember the time when we...?" When we had that flood, or got lost in the woods, or lost all our money on vacation? Do you remember that old house, that old school, do you remember the good old days? We were poorer, not richer, then. Or were we?

Every great school I know is in some old, badly heated and poorly furnished, dilapidated building. Every such school that has moved into a spanking new, clean, multi-million dollar building has lost its character and its camaraderie. John Locke went so far as to advise parents to give their children leaky shoes to walk to school in if they wanted their children to learn well! Suffering together builds togetherness, and if togetherness is more important for us and for our joy than freedom from suffering is, then God is good to allow this suffering.

There are two problems that remain. First, why do we need this painful treatment? Why must physical good be sacrificed to attain spiritual good? Why can't we learn wisdom and virtue without suffering? The Christian answer to that question is that we are fallen creatures, in an unnatural state, not in the state of nature. Sin has made us stupid, so that we can only learn the hard way. It is an answer you cannot prove or disprove. But it is an answer that fits the facts.

The second, harder problem that remains even if the principle of first and second things is used is the distribution of suffering. People get suffering thrown at them who apparently don't need it (good people like Job) and who apparently can't use it (like the cases at the beginning of this book). Pain embitters as often as it mellows.

The answer to this question must at least include the point that anyone can learn from suffering. We have free will. As Viktor Frankl says:

Do the prisoners' reactions to the singular world of the concentration camp prove that man cannot escape the influences of his surroundings? Does man have no choice of action in the face of such circumstances?

We can answer these questions from experience as well as on principle. The experiences of camp life show that man does have a choice of action. There were enough examples, often of a heroic nature, which proved that apathy could be overcome. . . . Man *can* preserve a vestige of spiritual freedom, of independence of mind, even in such terrible conditions of psychic and physical stress.

This is no cheap idealism. It comes from history's most horrible laboratory.

But the question still remains, why didn't God, foreseeing that some people would freely choose to respond to suffering with heroism and others with bitterness, withhold suffering from the latter? Perhaps we shall not know the answer to this question in this life. Perhaps we shall. But I doubt whether we will get the answer from the philosophers. It is time to move on from the area of general philosophical principles to concrete, individual cases, which seem more mysterious. Literature deals with such cases. So let's see what the poets and writers and artists say about this darker question.

FIVE

Seven Clues from the Artists

What is a Poet? A poet is an unhappy being whose heart is torn by secret sufferings, but whose lips are so strangely formed that when the sighs and the cries escape them, they sound like beautiful music. His fate is like that of the unfortunate victims whom the tyrant Phalais imprisoned in a brazen bull and slowly tortured over a steady fire: their cries could not reach the tyrant's ears so as to strike terror into his heart. When they reached his ears they sounded like sweet music. And men crowd about the poet and say to him: "Sing for us soon again"; that is as much as to say: "May new sufferings torment your soul, but may your lips be formed as before; the cries would only frighten us, but the music is delicious." And the critics come too and say: "Quite correct, and so it ought to be according to the rules of aesthetics." Now it is understood that a critic resembles a poet to a hair; he only lacks the suffering in his heart and the music upon his lips.

Kierkegaard

WHAT PLATO CALLS THE ANCIENT FEUD between philosophy and poetry is like the war between the sexes: a very silly war. Philosophy and poetry, like man and woman, are both necessary, unequal in nature, equal in value, and mutually dependent. Just as men are superior to women (at being men) and women are superior to men (at being women), so artists are superior to philosophers at art and philosophers are superior to artists at philosophy. And just as a world without men or without women would be half a world (and awfully dull), so a world without artists or without philosophers, without poets or without scientists, without inspiration or without intelligence, would be half a world (and awfully dull). Kant said that "concepts without sensations are empty, sensations without concepts are blind." Similarly, philosophy without art is empty, and art without philosophy is blind. The brain has two hemispheres and so does life. We turn now from left hemisphere to right. There are as many clues in this rich realm as in the other.

Clue One: Children's Stories—Suffering Makes You Real.

Children know some things adults don't, some primal, elemental things. One of these is that reality, or realness, is not a cut and dried thing. A child's metaphysics is in some ways subtler than an adult's. "To be or not to be, that is the question," says Hamlet. Poor Hamlet has lost his childhood. Children implicitly know that realness is a matter of degree and that it is somehow up to us, dependent on what we do, as co-creators. (Not that anything is real simply if you think so or want so, but that you can do something to make it realer.)

The velveteen rabbit in the classic of that title was more real than newer toys. Why? Because it suffered. Suffering makes you more real.

> "Real isn't how you are made," said the Skin Horse. "It's a thing that happens to you. When a child loves you for a long, long time, not just to play with, but REALLY loves you, then you become Real."
> "Does it hurt?" asked the Rabbit.
> "Sometimes," said the Skin Horse, for he was always truthful. "When you are Real you don't mind being hurt."

"Does it happen all at once, like being wound up," he asked, "or bit by bit?"

"It doesn't happen all at once," said the Skin Horse. "You become. It takes a long time. That's why it doesn't often happen to people who break easily, or have sharp edges, or who have to be carefully kept. Generally, by the time you are Real, most of your hair has been loved off, and your eyes drop out and you get loose in the joints and very shabby. But these things don't matter at all, because once you are Real you can't be ugly, except to people who don't understand."

The Little Prince, by Antoine de Saint Exupery, shows how we make things more real when we tame them; when we take responsibility for a thing, we give it a new, second life, a realer life, a life as part of our own. (This is what Heidegger calls *sorge,* or care; it is the essential mark of *dasein,* human existence.) The thing becomes a part of our life, as we can become part of God's when we let him do the same to us. The fox teaches the little prince this transcendental mystery:

"Come and play with me," proposed the little prince. "I am so unhappy."

"I cannot play with you," the fox said. "I am not tamed."

. . ."One only understands the things that one tames," said the fox. "Men have no more time to understand anything. They buy things all ready made at the shops. But there is no shop anywhere where one can buy friendship, and so men have no friends any more. If you want a friend, tame me."

"What must I do, to tame you?" asked the little prince.

"You must be very patient," replied the fox. . . .

So the little prince tamed the fox. And when the hour of his departure drew near—

"Ah," said the fox, "I shall cry."

"It is your own fault," said the little prince. "I never

wished you any sort of harm; but you wanted me to tame you . . ."

"Yes, that is so," said the fox.

"But now you are going to cry!" said the little prince.

"Yes, that is so," said the fox.

"Then it has done you no good at all!"

"It has done me good," said the fox. . . .

"It is the time you have wasted for your rose that makes your rose so important. . . . Men have forgotten this truth," said the fox. "But you must not forget it. You become responsible, forever, for what you have tamed. You are responsible for your rose . . ."

The rose, untamed, did not share in the sufferings of people. Tamed, it did. Perhaps we suffer so inordinately because God loves us so inordinately and is taming us. Perhaps the reason why we are sharing in a suffering we do not understand is because we are the objects of a love we do not understand.

Perhaps we are even becoming more real by sharing in sufferings that are the sufferings of God, both on earth, as part of Christ's work of salvation, and in heaven, as part of the eternal life of the Trinity which is the ecstatic death to self that is the essence of both suffering and joy. C.S. Lewis hints at this last high mystery in *The Problem of Pain*:

[In heaven] each soul, we suppose, will be eternally engaged in giving away to all the rest that which it receives. And as to God, we must remember that the soul is but a hollow which God fills. Its union with God is, almost by definition, a continual self-abandonment—an opening, an unveiling, a surrender, of itself. . . . We need not suppose that the necessity for something analogous to self-conquest will ever be ended, or that eternal life will not also be eternal dying. It is in this sense that, as there may be pleasures in hell (God shield us from them), there may be something not all unlike pains in heaven (God grant us soon to taste them).

For in self-giving, if anywhere, we touch a rhythm not only of all creation but of all being. For the Eternal Word also gives Himself in sacrifice; and that not only on Calvary. For when He was crucified He "did that in the wild weather of His outlying provinces which He had done at home in glory and gladness" (George Macdonald). From before the foundation of the world He surrenders begotten Deity back to begetting Deity in obedience.

From *The Little Prince* to the deepest secret of the eternal joy of the Trinity is a surprisingly short step.

Clue Two: Fairy Tales—Good Stories Need Monsters and Mystery.

We explore fairy tales as a distinct category from children's stories. As Tolkien pointed out, "the association of children and fairy-stories is an accident of our domestic history. Fairy-stories have in the modern lettered world been relegated to the 'nursery,' as shabby or old-fashioned furniture is relegated to the play-room, primarily because the adults do not want it, and do not mind if it is misused."

One of the best-known principles of fairy tales is that two ingredients necessary for a good story are monsters and mystery. Take, for instance, the tale told by Robert Farrar Capon in *The Third Peacock,* in answer to our question about God and suffering:

God has dangerously odd tastes: He is inordinately fond of risk and roughhouse. Any omnipotent being who makes as much room as he does for back talk and misbehavior strikes us as slightly addled. Why, when you're orchestrating the music of the spheres, run the awful risk of letting some fool with a foghorn into the violin section? Why set up the delicate balance of nature and then let a butcher with heavy thumbs mind the store? It just seems—well, *irresponsible*. If we were God we would be more serious and respectable: no freedom, no risks; just a smooth, obedient show presided over by an omnipotent bank president with a big gold watch.

At least so it seems, until you think about it. Then everything turns around and you are back on God's side before you know it. Try writing a fairy tale on the safe-and-sane view of the universe.

The princess is under the curse. She is asleep and cannot be awakened except by an apple from the tree in the middle of the garden at the Western End of the World. What does the king do? Well, on the theory that a well-run, no-risk operation makes the best of all possible worlds, he gets out his maps, briefs his generals, and sends a couple of well-supplied divisions to the garden to fetch the apple. It is only a matter of getting an odd prescription from an inconveniently located drugstore that doesn't deliver. He uses his power and does the job. The apple is brought to the palace and applied to the princess. She wakes up, eats breakfast, lunch, and dinner forever after and dies in bed at the age of eighty-two.

Everyone knows, of course, that that is not the way the story goes. To begin with, the garden isn't on any of the maps. Only one man in the kingdom, the hundred-year-old Grand Vizier, knows where it is. When he is summoned, however, he asks to be excused. It seems that he is scheduled to die later that evening and therefore cannot make the trip. He happens to have a map, but there is a complication. The map has been drawn with magical ink and will be visible only to the right man for the job. The king, of course, inquires how this man is to be found. Very simply, says the Vizier, he will be recognized by his ability to whistle in double stops and imitate a pair of Baltimore orioles accompanying each other at an interval of a minor third.

Needless to say, the king calls in his nobles, all of whom are excellent musicians. They whistle, sing, and chant at the paper, but nothing appears. They serenade it with airs to the lute and with pavanes played by consorts of recorders, sackbuts, shawms and rebecs, but still no luck. At last the king, in desperation, tells them to knock off for lunch and come back at two. He goes up on the parapet for a stroll and, lo and behold, what does he hear but somebody walking down the road whistling double stops like a pair of Baltimore orioles.

It is, of course, the Miller's Third Son, local school dropout and SDS member. The king, however, is not one to balk at ideologies when he needs help. He hauls the boy in, gives him the map and packs him off with a bag of Milky Ways and a six-pack of root beer. That night the boy reads the map. It seems pretty straightforward, except for a warning at the bottom in block capitals: AFTER ENTERING THE GARDEN GO STRAIGHT TO THE TREE, PICK THE APPLE AND GET OUT. DO NOT, UNDER ANY CIRCUMSTANCES, ENGAGE IN CONVERSATION WITH THE THIRD PEACOCK ON THE LEFT.

Any child worth his root beer can write the rest of the story for you. The boy goes into the garden and gets as far as the third peacock on the left, who asks him whether he wouldn't like a stein of the local root beer. Before he knows it, he has had three and falls fast asleep. When he wakes up, he is in a pitch-black cave; a light flickers, a voice calls—and from there on all hell breaks loose. The boy follows an invisible guide wearing a cocked hat and descends into the bowels of the earth; he rows down rivers of fire in an aluminum dinghy, is imprisoned by the Crown Prince of the Salamanders, finally rescued by a confused eagle who deposits him at the *Eastern* End of the World, works his way back to the Western End in the dead of winter, gets the apple, brings it home, touches it to the princess's lips, arouses her, reveals himself as the long lost son of the Eagle King and marries the princess. Then, and only then, do they live happily ever after.

Silly escapist fantasy, you say? Would you call the book of *Job* that? No? Well, then, the same clue to the mystery of suffering is there: the reason for the monsters and the mystery.

Reader: What? You mean just to make a good story? Is that why God lets us suffer? That's sadistic!

Author: Wait. Let me ask you a question, O.K.? In fact, make it eleven questions.

Reader: You have some nerve—asking me to sit still for not just one but eleven questions, after I just told you how impatient I was at your silly suggestion that we suffer because God puts us in a fairy tale!

Author: But you'll do it, because you're only a character in something less than a fairy tale. You're in my dialog.

Reader: And that's how you think it is in the real world too? We're just helpless puppets of God the omnipotent story-teller?

Author: No, we're not puppets. God is a better author than I am. He creates characters—real ones, not just imaginary ones. That's why we're really free, you see. God writes a story about free men and women, not about puppets. Now will you answer my eleven questions?

Reader: I have to. I'm at your mercy.

Author: Yes, you are. Now the first two questions are about stories in general. Then three questions about Capon's story, then three about the Job story, then three about a third story. Question one: If you were the author, which of Capon's two fairy tales would you write?

Reader: The second one, of course, the one with all the crazy stuff in it.

Author: The suffering, you mean.

Reader: It makes a better story, yes.

Author: And isn't it true that the thing we want and need and demand in our lives is to be in a good, a great, a meaningful story? To have our life have meaning?

Reader: Yes, but don't we want freedom from suffering too?

Didn't Freud prove that we're always motivated by the pleasure principle?

Author: No, he did not. He was wrong. People are willing to suffer for a reason, a cause, a meaning. That's simply a fact.

Reader: O.K., so I want to be in a meaningful story.

Author: Good; you just answered my second question.

Reader: But I don't understand why a story has to have suffering in it to be meaningful. You're comparing meaningful suffering with meaninglessness. Why not meaning without suffering?

Author: That was story one. You said it wasn't a very good story. No monsters and no mystery; no suffering and no ignorance; no frustration of desire and no frustration of mind.

Reader: I still don't understand . . .

Author: We're only up to clues, remember? We have pages and pages to go. One thing at a time. Not so fast.

Reader: Not so fast, indeed! I think I was too fast to agree with you in answering your second question. It's all very well for the author to choose an interesting story full of monsters and mystery and suffering, but not for the poor character. And that's us.

Author: Thank you. You just made me ask questions three, four, and five.

Reader: Why?

Author: To prove to you that your first answer to question two was correct.

Reader: I don't get it.

Author: Watch and you will. Here's question three. Imagine you were the character, the protagonist, the Miller's Third Son. You want the character's point of view; all right, you've got it. Now at the beginning of the tale, which tale would you choose to be in? You have the choice to avoid suffering and have your King get the apple for you, or to go into the second story, with all the monsters and mysteries.

Reader: Are you kidding? Who would choose the hard way if

they could get the same apple and princess the easy way? A straight line is the shortest distance between two points. That question tells for me, not for you.

Author: So it seems. But now question four. You're still the Miller's Third Son, but now you're in the middle of the second story, fighting with the Crown Prince of the Salamanders in the bowels of the earth. Are you glad you're in this story instead of the other one?

Reader: Silly question! Same answer. No way. Who wants to suffer?

Author: Ah, but to have suffered—perhaps that is another matter. So here's question five for you; you're the boy at the end of the tale. You've won the princess through your labors, through the craziness, and you can look forward to reminiscing about your adventures as you eat breakfast, lunch, and dinner with her for the next fifty years. You're a hero. Tell me, honestly, would you exchange having been in this story for having been in the other one?

Reader: No, to speak honestly. I see your point. But you have to go through all that suffering to get to that end.

Author: My point exactly. I rest my case.

Reader: Wait! That was a fairy tale. Real life isn't full of that kind of suffering: magic and heroic tasks to win a beautiful princess. It's full of dyings and disloyalties and dullnesses and despairs.

Author: Yes, it is. So let's talk about real life. Let's ask the same three questions about a realistic story, not a fairy tale. Let's take the story of Job. Here's question six: You're Job at the beginning of the story, good and happy and prosperous, sitting in the city gate solving everybody's problems, dispensing justice and wisdom and being the perfect example of the line from Psalm One which says, "How happy are the righteous!" Now God comes to you with a proposal. "Hey, Job, how would you like to move over to another story? Let me show you a preview. I've written (or at least inspired some unsuspecting poet to write) the script. See what you think of it." And he gives you the Book of Job. You begin to read it. Do you buy it?

Reader: No way! Who wants pirates to steal his fortune, terrorists to kill his kids, and his wife to call him a fool? Who wants to get boils all over, sit on a dung heap (do you know what a dung heap is?) scratching his sores with a potsherd, and be lectured to by three Howard Cosells about how wicked he must be? Who'd want to move from Psalm One to the Book of Job?

Author: Nobody. Right. Now the next question, question seven. You're Job in the middle of your story, sitting in your dung heap cursing the day of your birth, wondering where God has gone, philosophizing and getting all questions and no answers, weeping and wondering like crazy, trying to get those three pharisaical monkeys off your back. Are you glad you're in the Book of Job?

Reader: Same answer, of course. Nobody likes suffering.

Author: And now question eight, the point of it all. You're Job at the end of the story. Are you satisfied?

Reader: Certainly not!

Author: But Job was.

Reader: Why, for goodness' sake?

Author: Because he got his beautiful princess.

Reader: What do you mean?

Author: Do you remember how the story ends?

Reader: Not really.

Author: I'll tell you. God finally appears to Job. Job sees him face-to-face and is satisfied. He's happy because he's got his God back. His life has meaning.

Reader: I still don't get it. I wouldn't be satisfied yet.

Author: But Job was. That's the point. Job is glad to have been in his story. He's the character, not the author. In fact, God's whole point when he finally shows up is that Job is not the author, only the character. And Job accepts that and accepts his story. He's glad to have been in the Book of Job, the world's greatest classic of suffering.

Reader: I still don't understand why. Why?

Author: In a word, God.

Reader: You said before that we're willing to accept suffering only if we understand its meaning. But Job doesn't understand why he had to suffer, does he? God didn't explain anything to him, did he?

Author: No. But I didn't say we have to understand, just that we have to believe that our suffering has meaning. That's Job's position. He's not a hero of understanding, but a hero of faith.

Reader: Well, then I don't understand that.

Author: Neither did Job! Yet he believed, he accepted, he affirmed.

Reader: You say that Job is a realistic story, not a fairy tale! Well, that part of it is fairy tale to me.

Author: Then let's take the most realistic story of all—your life.

Reader: My life?

Author: Yes. Isn't that why we're in this dialog? To help you understand your life? Isn't that the reason the Book of Job was written? And Capon's fairy tale too?

Reader: I guess so.

Author: Don't you weep and wonder too?

Reader: Of course.

Author: Then answer these three questions about your life too. First, the "before" question, question nine: Before you were born, weren't you all nice and cozy and comfortable there in your mother's little womb? No suffering, right?

Reader: Right.

Author: If someone had presented you with the script for your life, the trauma of birth, of growing up, of disappointed love, of suffering, of sadness, of all the tragedies of your life, all the weeping and wondering, all the monsters and mystery, would you have chosen to be born? I ask that because that's really what those other two beginning questions were about, you know. Would the Miller's Third Son, would Job, would you have freely chosen to exit from your comfortable womb into a world with no guarantees except risk? Would you have exchanged total security for total insecurity?

Reader: No.

Author: How fortunate you were not consulted before you were born!

Reader: I suppose none of us would be here if we were.

Author: Exactly. How merciful of God to force us against our will into a world full of suffering!

Reader: I didn't say that.

Author: You've said the equivalent of it in practice.

Reader: In practice? How?

Author: You haven't committed suicide. You've decided, for whatever reason, or even for no reason, to live. And there's your tenth question. In the middle of the story that is your life, are you glad you're in it? You've answered yes by choosing to stay alive. You must believe you have more pluses than minuses in your life, because you could always move to zero, but you don't.

Reader: What strange things you show me about myself!

Author: And do you know why you make this strange choice to live?

Reader: No. I think I'm like Ivan Karamazov. "Love life more than the meaning of life, love life in spite of logic."

Author: Good for you.

Reader: That's good?

Author: That's what Ivan's brother Alyosha said. Ivan the atheist and Alyosha the Christian agreed there. They both loved life more than its meaning, loved whether they understood or not. Like Job. Like you.

Reader: Me too?

Author: Yes, because you're implicitly answering question eleven, the final and deciding question, with a resounding yes.

Reader: What's question eleven?

Author: The question from the point of view of the end of the story. Looking back at your life from the point of view of eternity, God's point of view, was it all worth it? Do you accept it, with all its suffering, as a package deal? Or would you exchange it for a womb, not to have been born?

Reader: I don't know anything about God's point of view. But from mine, now, I wouldn't exchange it for a womb, no.

Author: That's question ten, from in the middle of the story. You accept it. That's more heroic than the Miller's Third Son or Job.

Reader: That's because I don't have their sufferings.

Author: But you have your own. Yet you accept this life. Why?

Reader: I don't know why. I love life in spite of logic, like Ivan Karamazov.

Author: I think I know why.

Reader: Why?

Author: I think that even now you are unconsciously antici-pating the vision of eternity, the vision of the whole, the eucatastrophe that makes the whole story worthwhile.

Reader: Eucatastrophe?

Author: Tolkien's word. He calls it the highest function of the fairy tale.

Reader: I was talking about real life.

Author: Precisely. That's what fairy tales talk about too. Tolkien says:

> . . . the joy of the happy ending, or more correctly of the good catastrophe, the sudden joyous "turn" (for there is no true end to any fairy tale); this joy, which is one of the things which fairy stories can produce supremely well, is not essentially "escapist". . . . It does not deny the existence of *dyscatastrophe*, of sorrow and failure: the possibility of these is necessary to the joy of deliverance; it denies (in the face of much evidence, if you will) universal final defeat.

Reader: Justifying suffering by the happy ending sounds like hitting yourself on the head with a hammer because it feels so good when you stop.

Author: No. Joy is more than the relief of sorrow.

Reader: It still sounds to me like you're pulling out of the hat of the happy ending the impossible rabbit of an evil that is really good.

Author: Let me try to explain. Eucatastrophe means not just light but light out of darkness. That's more dramatic and more joyful than mere light. Job in chapter forty-two is more dramatic and more joyful than Job in chapter one. When God finally appeared to Job after so much silence and suffering, that was greater than God as Job's secure possession in the beginning. (And also truer, since God can never be anyone's possession.) When he appeared, he came out of the story, the whirlwind, the darkness, symbol of Job's suffering and mystery, weeping and wondering. Then Job really knew God, really appreciated him. And himself too.

It's like the boy in the bubble in chapter one: that last handclasp was infinitely precious. It was no ordinary handclasp. It was a universal symbol, the solution to war and all the world's problems. Out of the tragedy, we must touch each other in love. But we don't notice it unless it comes out of the bubble.

There was a dying sister in Ingmar Bergman's terrible movie *Cries and Whispers* who had every imaginable suffering. But during her last moment of real happiness, on a white swing in the yellow sunshine in the green yard, she says that this moment is worth anything, because this moment is all there is, this moment is eternal.

Reader: You're getting carried away. This is fantastic.

Author: Just the opposite. This is realistic, but we don't see it. Every moment is like that moment, but it takes the frame of darkness for us to realize the light. It takes the threat of death for us to appreciate life. Remember Emily in *Our Town*. Only when she saw those ordinary moments of life from the perspective of death did she appreciate them. She asked the Stage Manager, "Do any humans ever realize life while they live it?—every, every minute?" And he answered, "No. (Pause.) The saints and poets, maybe—they do some."

Reader: You mean we appreciate things only by contrast.

Author: Yes. Like a television screen; it looks grey until a picture comes on, and then the contrasting white makes the grey look black.

Reader: Why are we such fools? God doesn't need evil to appreciate good, does he?

Author: No. And we're not God.

Reader: But if God doesn't have to suffer to appreciate joy, then there's no necessary link between the two, as there is between left and right, or hot and cold. You can't imagine or conceive one of those without the other, but you can conceive of joy without suffering. That's what God is made of, isn't he?

Author: Sort of.

Reader: So joy without suffering is possible for God, therefore it is possible. Why isn't it possible for us?

Author: Good question.

Reader: Do you have a good answer?

Author: I think so. Even in the Garden of Eden, before there was sin and death and suffering, we were in time, we had to grow, to learn. But that was a joy. After we sinned, learning became a pain, because learning means submitting your mind to reality. That self-yielding was a pure joy in Eden, and it will be a pure joy again in heaven, and it's mostly a joy to the saints even now. But for most of us most of the time, yielding our self-will is painful.

Reader: Do you think there was anything interesting in Eden before sin came? Isn't sin necessary for drama? Wasn't Eden boring? What did they do, just eat all day?

Author: No, there was such drama that the whole of human happiness hung on one command, one fruit.

Reader: So if we hadn't sinned, there'd still be drama? But how can there be drama without suffering?

Author: There would still be drama, but of such a different nature that we can hardly imagine it and don't usually try. C.S. Lewis is almost the only exception, in *Perelandra*. And David Bolt in *Adam*. Drama isn't due to sin, or even necessarily due to suffering. Drama is good. There's drama in God. Even eternity, outside all time, is drama, eternal dynamism. Eternity isn't static or dull. If it were, heaven wouldn't be heaven. Only after sin did drama turn into tragedy, because we turned into tragedians. Only now do we get bored and jaded with happiness and need the contrast with suffering.

Reader: So the happy ending is joyful for us now only if there's unhappiness before it?

Author: Yes.

Reader: I still don't think that justifies all the atrocities that come before it. Do you?

Author: Of course I can't justify atrocities. Or explain them. Only eternity will totally solve the problem. That's the solution the Bible offers—that most realistic of books—and the one Aquinas gives in the *Summa,* quoting Augustine: "As Augustine says, 'Since God is the highest good, He would not allow any evil to exist in His works unless His omnipotence and goodness were such as to bring good even out of evil.' This is part of the infinite goodness of God, that He should allow evil to exist and out of it produce good."

Reader: That sounds like a fairy tale answer, all right.

Author: Right. It's very realistic.

Reader: I was being sarcastic.

Author: But I wasn't. Scripture, like fairy tales, is like life. For one thing, it's a story, not a formula. And it's the only complete story. The King in *Alice in Wonderland* gives the White Rabbit a three-part direction on how to tell a story. He says, "Begin at the beginning, and go on till you come to the end, then stop." The Bible is the only book that perfectly follows this direction.

Reader: I think we should stop now, even though we haven't come to the end. It's been a long dialog.

Author: Yes, it has. Thank you for listening. And for talking back. I hope other readers do the same.

Clue Three: The Myths—Paradise Lost

Myth does not mean lie or even fiction; myth means thinking in pictures rather than abstract concepts. Especially thinking in moving pictures, pictures that move in time and tell a story (*mythos* means literally story) and pictures that move us to respond. Something deep in us says yes to the myths even as our reason and common sense say no. The world thought mythically for many, many millenia; only recently, only for the last 2,400 years since the Greeks taught us to think rationally, and only for the last 4,000 years since the Jews taught us to think ethically, have we earthlings ever thought about the deepest issues in our lives in any other way than mythically.

Folklorists and anthropologists, who help us overcome our historical provincialism and our chronological snobbery by investigating and taking seriously these ancient stories, have found that certain themes recur in all or nearly all the world's myths. Father Heaven and Mother Earth, sacred time and space, ritual language, initiation rites, a universal flood, the gods designing the world (*creating* is the wrong word; the idea of a creation of the entire universe out of nothing is a uniquely Jewish idea)—these and other themes are found in East and West, North and South, island and continent, big and little tribes, very old and very new. And one of the most persistent and universal themes is the answer the myths give to the mystery of suffering.

The answer is a myth, i.e., a mystery. A mystery-question is answered by a mystery-answer. Deep calls to deep, for the myths come from a deep place in us. Psychologists, especially Jungians, have discovered something even more amazing than the consistency of mythic themes throughout the world: the consistency of myths with dreams. We still dream in myth. Our conscious mind has forgotten myth and perhaps scorned it, but our unconscious, deeper mind has not.

What do the myths and dreams say about the mystery of suffering and the two associated mysteries of death and injustice (bad things happening to good people)? Essentially the same thing as the familiar story in Genesis. They say something almost no one in the world but orthodox Jews and Christians believe any more: that suffering and death and injustice all came into the world late, by a fall, or fault, or accident on our part; that we were originally innocent, happy, and immortal; that we brought suffering into the world; that we remember paradise lost.

Why does this idea feel so incredible to the modern mind? Because science knows nothing of it. Not because science has disproved it, because it hasn't. In other words, we have an unscientific attitude toward science, a religious attitude toward science. There is no scientific proof that only scientific proofs are good proofs; no way to prove by the scientific method that the scientific method is the only valid method. So let's be scientific and open-minded and consider the myth. A scientific attitude examines all available evidence. Is there evidence for the truth of the paradise lost myth?

Physically, no. There are no fossil remains of Eden, no historical documents from paradise. The core of Adam's apple is not in any museum. But we do have evidence from another quarter. We *feel* like exiled kings, fallen Adams, paradise-losers. Pascal says:

> What is nature in animals we call wretchedness in man, thus recognizing that, if his nature is today like that of the animals, he must have fallen from some better state which was once his own. Who indeed would think himself unhappy not to be king except one who had been dispossessed? . . . Who would think himself unhappy if he had

only one mouth, and who would not if he had only one eye? It has probably never occurred to anyone to be distressed at not having three eyes, but those who have none are inconsolable.

If man had never been corrupted, he would, in his innocence, confidently enjoy both truth and felicity, and, if man had never been anything but corrupt, he would have no idea either of truth or bliss. But unhappy as we are, we have an idea of happiness but we cannot attain it.

We seem to dimly remember perfection, for we judge imperfections by this standard. We seem to have fallen from paradise, for we do not find this world enough; we are not content and resigned to suffering, injustice, and death. Animals are. They try to escape these evils, of course, but they are not scandalized by them. They make no idealistic demands. They simply accept. We do not (despite the advice of our pagan or animalistic psychologists). We have a divine discontent, a lover's quarrel with the world. To have a quarrel with *here*, to criticize *here*, you need to know *there* as a standard. If the only world we ever knew or remembered was *here*, we would feel at home here. We do not. Therefore . . . the paradise lost myth.

I do not claim that the above argument proves the historical truth of the myth of paradise lost. Nor do I claim that the universality of the myth proves it true. But these are certainly two powerful clues, and to ignore them or to scorn them sounds suspiciously like a cover-up.

The paradise lost myth connects two things we do not usually connect: sin and suffering, sin and death. It explains suffering (which is a thousand little deaths) and death (the big suffering) by (1) tracing them to a historical cause, (2) identifying the cause as us ("we have met the enemy and they is us," in the words of Pogo, one of America's great philosophers), rather than God or nature, and (3) seeing justice rather than injustice in suffering; it is punishment for sin. More, it is the inevitable and necessary punishment for sin, as broken bones are the inevitable and necessary punishment for jumping off a cliff. What the myth does not explain is the distribution of suffering to individuals. For myth works on the universal level, the general and racial level.

But we exist on this level too, as well as on the individual level, though we may forget this. Therefore myth, for us, is relevant and realistic, not sheer fantasy and escapism. *I* am part of *we*, and *we* have sinned, have disobeyed and divorced ourselves from the source of all life and joy, therefore fallen into death and suffering, lifelessness and joylessness, the opposites of the God we have run from. The myth, though strange, explains the equally strange fact of our penchant for self-destructive behavior. It is like a strangely shaped thing, a key, that opens another strangely shaped thing, a lock. The lock is not just suffering but our outrage at it. The myth says that we suffer and find this outrageous, we die and find this natural fact unnatural, because we dimly remember Eden. We are orphaned children, separated lovers, disinherited princes, homeless wanderers, like Gilgamesh, Ulysses, Aeneas. The heroes of the old myths tell us who we are.

Clue Four: Greek Drama—Wisdom through Suffering

Our fourth clue from the artists comes from Greek drama. (The Greeks gave us nearly everything worth giving except for the one thing necessary, which the Jews gave us.) It is a very simple, very well-known, and very often forgotten point: that from suffering comes wisdom.

The Book of Job is a typical Greek tragedy in this respect, though not in its literary form. Aeschylus expresses the wisdom through suffering theme poignantly:

Day by day
Bit by bit

Pain drips upon the heart
As against our will
And even in our own despite
Comes wisdom
From the awful grace of the gods.

Rabbi Abraham Heschel puts the point as simply as it can be put. "The man who has not suffered—what does he know anyway?"

Consider the following syllogism:

If we do not suffer, we are not wise.
If we are not wise, we are not blessed.
Therefore if we do not suffer, we are not blessed.

Nearly everyone will agree with the first premise. Not everyone, however, agrees with the conclusion, because not everyone agrees with the second premise. This is because not everyone can distinguish blessedness from happiness, objective perfection from subjective satisfaction, true happiness from happy feelings, real needs from wants. If anyone identifies happiness with blessedness, the conclusion of our syllogism sounds simply silly: that if we do not suffer unhappiness, we are not happy.

The conclusion of the argument, however, follows from its two premises. If you admit the first and the second, you must admit the third, the conclusion. Since you probably do not deny the first, you must deny the second. That is, you must see wisdom as a nonessential factor in blessedness. In other words, for this lesson from Greek tragedy to be any sort of answer to the mystery of suffering, it must be assumed that wisdom is very valuable—more valuable, in fact, than comfort or pleasure or freedom from suffering.

It is easy to see and admit this when we are not suffering. But it is much harder to see when our minds are blinded by pain. One of the worst things pain does is turn our eyes inward, to ourselves. Sick people often say that the worst thing about being sick is that it makes you so self-centered. But that certainly isn't wisdom. Our so-called clue seems to be two-faced.

Perhaps the resolution of our dilemma is that suffering leads to wisdom in the long run but not in the short run, and that short-range folly is a price worth paying for long-range wisdom. Job, the classic sufferer, admits that his pain makes his words unwise: "My suffering is more than I can bear. What wonder then that my words are wild?" Yet Job learned from his suffering and from his folly. (Yes, folly. We are all fools, and no one more than one who thinks he is not.) And we can learn too. In the end, as we saw in our fairy tale, we ourselves, like Job, admit that it was worth it.

But why is it worth it? Why is wisdom worth suffering for? Why is wisdom worth more than pleasure? Why is foolishness worse than pain?

Because of what we are. We are not animals. We are human beings, with minds, souls, spirits, wills, psyches. Wisdom is the food of our souls. Without it, we starve. Just as hunters make sacrifices and endure suffering in order to capture their prey and get food to survive, so do we philosophers, we hunters of wisdom, that far more elusive and far more precious quarry.

But why is it necessary to sacrifice? Why do we learn wisdom only the hard way, by suffering? Why are we such poor learners, such fallen creatures?

Here the paradise lost story comes in. The clues are beginning to fit together and make up a coherent picture. Whether the picture is true or not is up to you to decide. But the picture is not yet complete. It has no capstone.

Clue Five: Science Fiction—Freedom vs. Happiness

Science fiction is modern man's new mythic literature. Many of the same images and many of the same themes occur spontaneously in this new mythic form as in the old. Forgotten to consciousness, they are not forgotten to the great collective unconscious, which this genre pulls on more than others.

One of these themes, one of the most popular in all of science fiction, is the anti-utopian theme: a futuristic society that has abolished suffering by technology, cured disease, abolished war and poverty, controlled accidents, sometimes even conquered death by artificial immortality. In these stories, such a society is always a colossal fake: apparently happy, but experiencing deep failure; apparently humane, but really inhuman. The abolition of suffering turns out to be the abolition of humanity.

Probably the most famous example is *Brave New World*, "a streamlined, soulless Eden" (the only publisher's blurb I have ever remembered) where there is no Beethoven, no Shakespeare, no da Vinci, and no suffering. "Everybody's happy now," is the fundamental argument for *Brave New World*. If you're bored, there's the endlessly fascinating game of centrifugal bumble-puppy; if you're upset, there's the wonder drug soma ("a gramme is better than a damn"), and of course there's plenty of free love, or rather free sex. Motherhood, childbirth, and families are regarded as obscene and inefficient. The sources of suffering are all dried up. The characters in *Brave New World* are happy because they are part puppet, part animal, and part vegetable. The only human character, John, the savage from an Indian reservation, can maintain his humanity and his sanity only by suffering and death, and since his brave new world gives him no opportunity for either, he is driven to self-flagellation and finally suicide. The theme of the book is so strange that when it is voiced naked it sounds like pure paradox, but so true that when it is experienced inherent in the story it is compelling. It is that we need to suffer to remain human. Like any good novel, it presents its truth rather than explaining it or arguing for it, but truth it is.

Another science fiction novel with the same theme, nearly as famous as *Brave New World*, is Arthur C. Clarke's *Childhood's*

End. In this novel, a benevolent, advanced race of extra-terrestrials imposes peace on earth by force. The result, years later, is a world so perfect, so boring, and so meaningless that suicide is (again) the "consummation devoutly to be wished."

What's missing in such an anti-utopia is not just suffering but also the thing that makes suffering possible, freedom. Freedom is also the thing that makes suffering meaningful. Freedom is thus both the source and the solution to suffering.

The choice in such stories is between freedom and happiness. Everyone wants both, of course; yet the two are in tension, often in contradiction. Which is more important? We want happiness more, but we need freedom more. We are fools because we put the second thing first. If our foolishness is allowed to succeed and to build a brave new world, we abolish our humanity.

The pilot show for "Star Trek" culminated in such a choice. Captain Pike, prematurely aged and paralyzed, is offered the choice between freedom and happy slavery in a kind of space zoo as a specimen to be studied by the great brains who rule the forbidden planet Talus IV. Their physical power is small but they wield great hypnotic mental powers and they promise to give Captain Pike nothing but happy dreams for the rest of his life. While he is in fact only an old man in a cage, he will think he has a young, healthy body and is having wonderful adventures on other worlds slaying monsters and loving a beautiful young woman (who is really a wrinkled old hag). Which shall he choose, freedom or happiness? The real world of suffering and truth or the illusionary world of happy dreams?

The original plot called for him to choose freedom, but it was changed for television, and he chose happiness instead, without even any hesitation—implying that the writer assumed that every normal viewer would find his choice as natural and necessary as the writer did. After all, who would think freedom to know the truth and live in the real world worth suffering for?

An old "Twilight Zone" episode took the opposite position from this writer. In the first scene, a gang of bank robbers is trapped by the police, refuses to surrender, and is shot. The protagonist falls in a pool of blood, blacks out, and wakes to find himself walking on fluffy white clouds at the golden gate of a celestial city. A black-bearded, white-robed old man with a kindly look takes him in and offers him whatever he desires. But he's soon bored with the free gold, which can't buy anything (everything is free). His partners, he is told, are in "the other place," and even the beautiful girls are boring because they only laugh when he tries to hurt them (he has a sadistic streak). He summons the St. Peter figure. "There must be some mistake." "No, we make no mistakes here." "Can't you send me back to earth?" "Of course not. You're dead." "Well then, I must belong with my friends in the Other Place. Send me there." "Oh, no, we can't do that. Rules, you know." "What is this place, anyway?" "This is the place where you get everything you want." "But I thought I was supposed to *like* heaven." "Heaven? Who said anything about heaven? Heaven is the Other Place."

Again, a world without suffering appears more like hell than like heaven.

The greatest and most famous of all freedom vs. happiness stories is not technically science fiction, but fantasy. It is the story within a story in Dostoyevski's *Brothers Karamazov,* titled "The Grand Inquisitor." Jesus returns to earth again in the middle of the Spanish Inquisition. Torquemada, the Grand Inquisitor, confronts him and tells him he will burn him at the stake tomorrow and the people will love him for it, just as they wanted him crucified the first time he came. Jesus, who has the reputation for kindness, is really cruel, says the Inquisitor, because he expects of everyone what only the strong can endure: freedom of conscience, naked before God, freely choosing between good and evil. The Grand Inquisitor, on the other hand, the man who has the reputation for being cruel, is really kind, because he takes from the people the intolerable burden of freedom that Christ gave them. Christ suffers, and so do his followers, because of this gift of freedom (i.e., free choice, free will). The Inquisitor forbids free choice and free thought by burning heretics, and in so doing he relieves the people of the greatest cause of their suffering, freedom.

Such a program, says the Inquisitor, was the worldly wisdom of the Devil's three temptations in the wilderness, and Jesus was a fool to say no to the use of force to compel belief by miracle, mystery, and authority, thus making mankind one happy, harmonious, uniform ant-heap. The Inquisitor's argument is surprisingly strong because he speaks not only from the pages of a fantasy or from the pages of history, but from some of the corners of our own hearts. Jesus answers him not a word, as God answered Job with not a straight word, not a reason. Instead, he kisses the Inquisitor, and the Inquisitor shudders at that kiss.

Christ's love makes us shudder. It shatters us with tenderness. Love somehow goes with suffering. Freedom goes with suffering. Truth, wisdom, knowledge of reality, go with suffering. It seems that everything that has intrinsic value, everything that cannot be bought or negotiated or compromised or relativized or reduced, goes with suffering.

Creation is another such thing. We look next at the connection between suffering and the act of creation.

Clue Six: Creative Artists—Birth Pangs

Nearly everyone knows that artists are supposed to suffer, but not everyone knows why. It is the same reason mothers suffer in giving birth. All artists are mothers. To be an artist is to be a creator, whether of a symphony or a supper or a painting or a person. Motherhood is the primary art, the art of creating (procreating) people.

Creation involves suffering. That is obvious. But why this should be so is not so obvious. Is it a necessity rooted in the very nature of things? To make an omelet you have to break some eggs? Or is it an unnatural situation? Animals do not have pain in childbirth, as we do. According to Genesis, this pain was one of the results of the Fall.

Whatever the reason, for us as we are now, creation involves suffering, and the greatest creativity involves the greatest suffering. The greatest beauty comes from the greatest suffering. Tragedy is our highest literary form. Sad music is the most beautiful music.

Not everyone creates an external work of art, like a painting or a book, but everyone creates an internal work of art, a life, a real-life story. Everyone also creates a character, a person: themselves. God gives us only the raw material; by our choices we shape it into who we are. The primary creative task of every person is becoming themselves. We are always painting our own eternal self-portrait. Each choice is a brush stroke. We are sculpting our own likeness. Each act is a cut of the chisel. And since everyone is an artist and artists must suffer, therefore everyone must suffer. Saints suffer most because they are the greatest artists of all.

Clue Seven: The Poets—Death as a Lover and Death as Birth

The deepest clue of all comes from the seers, the visionaries. A true poet is a seer, and not just a sayer, a wordsmith. A true poet is a mystic. He makes the unseen seen, expresses the unexpressed, bends words beyond themselves to point to what is beyond words, to the mystical. The clue that we find in these poets and mystics boldly plunges our astonished eyes into the deepest and darkest kind of suffering—death—and then sees a light in this very heart of darkness.

Death is in a sense pure suffering, pure diminishment. As Teilhard de Chardin put it, "In death as in an ocean all our slow or swift diminishments flow out and merge. Death is the sum and consummation of all our diminishments." But in the heart of death the visionaries find life and birth. Looked at deeply and unflinchingly enough, death appears as a door, not a hole; and the other side of this darkest door is the purest light. Death appears as a mother, birthing us from a dim little womblike world (this universe) into a world of incredibly larger dimensions and unimagined splendors. Death becomes our birth canal, our passageway to life. What philosophers argue for and theologians believe, visionaries see.

There are over eight million ordinary people in America alone who have had a "near-death experience" and shared some part of this vision, this experience—not mere reason, not even mere belief, but experience—of life beyond death. At the border, from a distance, "through a glass, darkly," always inadequately (they all insist that their words are utterly inadequate), they have seen through death to life and light and love, the three eternal verities. They usually meet a "being of light" and feel totally known and totally loved by him. This near-death experience is so commonly known by now largely because of the pioneering work of Elizabeth Kubler-Ross (*On Death and Dying*) and Raymond Moody (*Life After Life*). However you interpret the experience, it is there. Eight million mystics!

Death becomes for them more (but not less) than the enemy that it naturally appears to be at first, and more than the stranger we turn it into by denial; something more even than the friend that a merely psychological acceptance of death makes it into, a merely stoical resignation to necessity (Freud's "we must make friends with the necessity of dying"). It becomes something exultant: a mother, a birth process, and even, finally, a lover, or the instrument of a lover, the golden chariot sent by the divine king to fetch his Cinderella bride from the ashes and cinders of death to take her to his great castle to live and love with him forever.

If—somehow—all suffering were connected with that, and if we had even an inkling and a desperate hope of that, then that would make suffering infinitely worthwhile. Even the most horrible life on earth would be only a difficult birth.

It seems as if we are being moved, pushed, tugged, as by a

great undertow, out to sea, to the deeps, to him. We have explored two of the three kinds of prophets (philosophers and artists) that seem to point to him from a distance. We turn now to the most familiar kind of prophet, the moralists of the chosen people, of which he was one. We are getting dangerously close.

SIX

Eight Clues from the Prophets

*"Behold, I am about to do a thing in Israel, at which the two
ears of everyone that hears it will tingle."*
                                            1 Samuel 3:11

PROPHET MEANS MOUTH, or mouthpiece, one who speaks for
another. Prophets speak for God. If we want God's answers to
our questions rather than just our own answers (and who but a
fool wouldn't?), we must go to the prophets.

By the prophets we usually mean the Jewish prophets of the
Old Testament. I have said that the philosophers and poets are
prophets too, mouthpieces of God. But the primary prophets
are the moralists, especially the familiar Old Testament
figures. They are primary not because they alone are specifically chosen by God—who but God chose Socrates or
Shakespeare?—but because they are specially certified by God,
guaranteed by God. Their truth is authoritative, unmixed with
falsehood.

They are closer to God than the philosophers or artists in
that they have a more face-to-face relationship with him. They
may not be as intelligent as the philosophers or as sensitive as
the artists, but they stand closer to the center of the divine fire.
Of the three great ideals, the three divine attributes (the true,

the good, and the beautiful), they specialize in the central, the primary one, goodness.

Yet they are not close enough, not final. They see the answer from afar. Their solution is future. Though essentially forth-tellers, they are also fore-tellers (the popular meaning of the word *prophet*). They are still at a distance from the definitive answer to the darkest of mysteries. But that distance is in the same dimension as the problem: the dimension of history. They are on the same road, but "down the road apiece."

By the way, though I believe the truth of the prophets' words (and of everything in the Bible, as God's word), I do not assume this here. This journey of exploration is undertaken as a thought-experiment. That is the nature of clues; they neither assume the truth of a conclusion, nor do they prove it, but they point to it and leave us free to follow or to turn aside.

Clue One: Moses—Who Started It?

Moses, or whoever wrote Genesis, tells the beginning, or genesis, of the story of the origin of suffering in sin, in the fall of Adam, who is both an individual and all mankind, i.e., also ourselves. We suffer because we sin. And the connection is necessary and natural. It was not that God got mad when Adam disobeyed, and said, "Take that, you cad!" It was not like Mommy slapping Baby's hand when Baby took the cookies. It was like getting sick when you eat poison. It was like a chain of three iron rings suspended from a magnet. The magnet represents God, the source of all life. Magnetism represents life. The three rings represent the soul, the body, and the world, or nature. When the first ring is attached to the magnet (i.e., when man's soul adheres to God), the whole chain is magnetized together (there is harmony). But once Adam declares independence from God (sin), the whole chain falls apart; death, the alienation between soul and body, and suffering, the alienation between body and world, necessarily follow from sin, the alienation between soul and God.

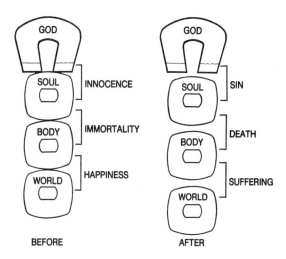

All three evils, sin and death and suffering, are from us, not from God; from our misuse of our free will, from our disobedience. We started it!

There is another clue in the story in Genesis. God does not abandon us to our deserved fate but immediately begins the long restoration program that is the main (though hidden) point of our history. Genesis 3:15 is the first announcement of God's solution, the first prophecy in the Bible. God says to Satan,

"I will put enmity between you and the woman,
and between your seed and her seed;
he shall bruise your head,
and you shall bruise his heel."

It promises a Messiah who, at the cost of his own heel, or weak spot, will destroy the head, or stronghold, or power of evil. The seed of the woman, Eve's own great-great-great-etc.-grandson Jesus, by becoming a man born from a woman (Mary, the new Eve), will destroy these three destructions, sin and death and suffering, and restore to human nature three levels of life: spiritual life (vs. sin), eternal life (vs. death) and even the life of freedom from suffering.

But when he came the first time, he did not apparently do any of this. People still sinned, died, and suffered. He too suffered and died, but did not sin. But we still suffer, still die, and still sin. Is he a failure then?

No, he is an actor in the play in time, a hero in the battlefield that takes time to win. The king has landed, and the battle has begun, but it is not over. In a sense it is—"it is finished"—but the mop-up operation takes a while. The play is only in act three or four. He came the first time to buy the land and dig the foundation, his own humanity. He will come a second time to build his house on it. In that house there will be no medicine cabinet, no first aid equipment, for there will be no more suffering. God "will wipe away every tear from their eyes" (Rv 21:4).

Clue Two: Abraham—Faith Suffers.

Abraham is the first Jew. The Jews are history's strangest people. By every known law of history, the Jews should have perished many times already. Pharaoh, Nebuchadnezzar, Caesar, the Turks, the Christians, the Muslims, Hitler, their own obstinacy—none of these have been able to effect "a final solution to the Jewish problem." For they are a problem, both to the mind (we don't understand why they survive and thrive) and to the will (as the collective conscience of the human race, they gave us the great gift of guilt).

The puzzle of their survival can be solved by solving the other, parallel puzzle of their beginning. They survive by the same agency and for the same purpose as they began, and we can see both in Abraham. The bottom line is that they began in divine providence, their survival agency was divine providence, and their purpose was divine providence. They were to be God's instrument to save the entire world from sin and death and suffering. They are the main road through the jungle of history. Look at them to see what God is up to.

It sounds strange to find the solution to sin, death, and suffering among the people whose own records, which they have carefully and lovingly preserved, condemns them as obstinate sinners, whose death has been desired and plotted by more tyrants than any, and who are more famous for suffering than any other people. (To quote a line from the movie *My Favorite Year*, "Jews are great at two things: suffering, and finding great Chinese restaurants.") If, as their records claim, they are God's chosen people, they are chosen not for privilege but for suffering. Like Jesus!

But their suffering is for a reason, for a purpose. The prophetic spirit of the Jews finds a meaning and a purpose in history, thereby transforming mankind's understanding of history. Their genius for finding meaning everywhere—for example, in science and the world of nature—can be explained in only two ways: either they were simply smarter than anyone else, or it was God's doing, not theirs. The notion of the chosen people is really the humblest possible interpretation of their history.

The application of the Jewish penchant for finding meaning to the mystery of suffering is what leads a man like Viktor Frankl to speak these ringing words from the depths of a Nazi death camp:

> If there is a meaning in life at all, then there must be a meaning in suffering. Suffering is an ineradicable part of life.
> I was struggling to find the reason for my sufferings, my slow dying. In a last violent protest against the hopelessness of imminent death, I sensed my spirit piercing through the enveloping gloom. I felt it transcend that hopeless, meaningless world, and from somewhere I heard a victorious "Yes" in answer to my question of the existence of an ultimate purpose.

Man's main concern is not to gain pleasure or to avoid pain, but rather to see a meaning in his life. That is why man is even ready to suffer, on the condition, to be sure, that his suffering has a meaning.

How did the Jews begin? By the call of Abraham about 4,000 years ago. "O.K., time to go," says God to Abraham as he was later to say to Job and still later to his own Son. "Time to leave your comfort, security, and happiness there in Ur in Chaldea, that civilized and cultured city. Out into the wilderness, to a land I shall show you. Out into suffering and insecurity and darkness and blind faith. You will fall flat on your face many times because you will be looking at the darkness I'm sending you into rather than at the light of my face and my words to you. But I will not give up on you, ever. From you shall come a people and a person in whom all the nations of the earth will be blessed eternally. You are the father of the mother of the Savior. You are the father of the womb, the people, the soil in which I shall plant my seed of salvation. It shall be a salvation from suffering and death through suffering and death. Now—go. Begin."

Poor Abraham! Poor Sarah, when Abraham told her God had commanded him to leave their mansion in suburban Ur and become campers in nowhere. Deservedly has Abraham been called the father of the faithful.

And then the Isaac incident, the worst suffering of all. God asks for dear Isaac back, the one Abraham loved more dearly than anyone or anything except God. Read Kierkegaard's little masterpiece on this incident, *Fear and Trembling,* to plumb some of the depths of Abraham's suffering. That suffering was not mainly physical but spiritual. It was the suffering and death of the ego, the self-will, and the human reason; the suffering of a good, strong-minded, and strong-willed man who had the wisdom to "trust in the Lord with all your heart, and lean not on your own understanding" (Prv 3:5). God's way out of the mess seemed to lead further into the mess. God's solution to suffering was to call a man and a people into exile, into wilderness, into suffering. The solution to suffering was to suffer more!

Clue Three: Samuel—Suffering Speeds History's Cycle.

Samuel is the prophet who probably wrote many of the historical books of the Old Testament (1 and 2 Samuel, 1 and 2 Kings, and perhaps Judges). Samuel is the historian of the Old Testament.

The long story from Abraham to Jesus, which is recorded in the Bible, and the continuation of that story for 2,000 more years since Jesus, which is the story of the history of Israel, is like one large object lesson. Other peoples and nations have histories too, of course. But Israel's history is written large for all the world to see because it is like a mirror. In it we can see the principle that explains and that is at work in the history of all other nations: Greece, Rome, England, Germany, the United States.

The Greeks, in fact, discovered the second half of the principle. The principle is that a people goes through stages or cycles in which six parts can be distinguished. Let's begin with suffering, since that's the beast we are questing after. The stages then are: (1) Suffering, (2) Repentance, (3) Blessedness, (4) Luxury (*koros*), (5) Pride (*hybris*), (6) Disaster (*ate*).

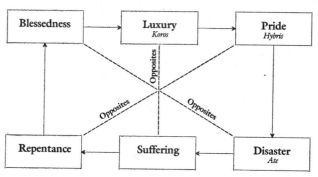

The meaning and purpose of suffering in history is that it leads to repentance. Only after suffering, only after disaster, does Israel, do nations, do individuals turn back to God (stage two, repentance). Suffering brings repentance. We learn the hard way. As C.S. Lewis says, "God whispers in our pleasures but shouts in our pains. Pain is his megaphone to rouse a dulled world."

Repentance then leads to blessedness, since God is the source of all joy, all life, all good. The principle is not arbitrary or changeable. God couldn't have made it different. He couldn't have given us blessedness without repentance because there can never be any such thing for fallen creatures. As C.S. Lewis says, "If we will not learn to eat the only fruit the universe can grow—the only fruit any possible universe can grow—we must starve eternally."

Then, alas, the blessedness does not last. We are fallen creatures; when we are not climbing to God, we are falling away from him. When we are not turning to him, we are turning away. Our blessedness becomes luxury, self-indulgence, comfort and security mongering. This is where the Greeks step in. Their philosophy of history sees the last three stages: luxury (*koros*) leads to pride (*hybris*), which leads to disaster (*ate*). Jesus' parable of the rich man says the same thing:

> And he told them a parable, saying, "The land of a rich man brought forth plentifully; and he thought to himself, 'What shall I do, for I have nowhere to store my crops?' And he said, 'I will do this; I will pull down my barns, and build larger ones; and there I will store all my grain and my goods. And I will say to my soul, Soul, you have ample goods laid up for many years; take your ease, eat, drink, be merry.' But God said to him, 'Fool! This night your soul is required of you; and the things you have prepared, whose will they be?' So is he who lays up treasure for himself, and is not rich toward God." (Lk 12:16-21)

We turn blessings from God into the attempt to be as blessed as God and even into the arrogant demand to play God, to say, "I am the master of my fate, I am the captain of my soul." Jews and Greeks alike know that "pride goes before destruction, and a haughty spirit before a fall" (Prv 16:18). Overstepping our bounds, we fall off the cliff into the abyss.

What the pessimistic Greeks did not know was the hopeful and optimistic half of the cycle. (The Greeks here stand for all the pagans, all the Gentiles, all the nations except the Jews.) The Greeks had a devolutionary, pessimistic philosophy of history. Their golden age was always in the past. Only the Jews had an evolutionary, hopeful, progressive philosophy of history. Their golden age was in the future, in "the day of the Lord," which we shall explore next. The Greeks have the reputation for being the sunny optimists, the happy humanists, and the Jews have the reputation for being the finger-wagging moralists, doomsters, and pessimists. But it is really the other way round on the deepest level. The Jews' moralism was deeply optimistic. If there was a road to disaster, viz., pride, there was also a road from disaster, viz., repentance. And ultimately, God and goodness would triumph.

The Jews could be suspicious and narrow and pessimistic about many little things because they were so optimistic and positive about one big thing: the person in charge. The Greeks may have been optimistic about many little human things, but they were deeply pessimistic about everything. Their "god of everything" was called Pan, and his work was pandemonium. And over all the gods ruled the dark power of *moira*, blind fate. The Greeks lived in a little world of light surrounded by an enormous ultimate darkness. Their distinctive expression was tragedy. The Jews lived in a world of darkness surrounded by light. Their distinctive expression was prophecy. The Greeks begin in life and light and leisure and end in death and darkness and suffering. The Jews begin in darkness and suffering and point out of it to a great light. "The people who walked in darkness have seen a great light" (Is 9:2).

The darkness is great indeed, not only of suffering but of sin. The history of Israel is largely a history of failures. The Old Testament is a record of repeated failures. It's incredible—just think, here is God's own chosen people, so bad that time and time again there is left hardly anyone in Israel who loves and worships God. Do you think the world is bad now, that there are few true believers, and that the power of evil is very great? Well, read the Old Testament and you will come away grateful to God for such a godly world as the one we live in.

The record is dismal. Only a few good kings among dozens of deeply wicked ones. Goodness is the exception, evil the rule. The history of Israel looks like a few candles in a crypt. And so does the history of the world, for which Israel is a mirror. The most realistic stories are tragedies.

And yet disaster and tragedy is not the end. There is turning. Suffering's historical purpose, in the history of Israel, in the world, and in individuals, is to lead from disaster, not to it. Suffering is a road out, a road to repentance, which is the door to blessedness.

But not all suffering is punishment for sin. Not all suffering is deserved. Good people suffer too, people who do not need a kick in the pants to repent. Why does God allow them to suffer so much?

The prophets of Israel answer this question in two ways, and we shall explore these answers more completely later in the book. Briefly, they are, first, that even good people need repentance, and the better they are, the more they see and say this. It is the saints who say they are the greatest sinners. The second is that the good suffer not only for themselves but for others. We shall examine also this mysterious idea of vicarious atonement later.

Clue Four: Jeremiah—There Are No Good People.

Jeremiah is called the weeping prophet. Tender-hearted and sensitive, he wept over the sins of his city, just as Jesus would do centuries later. We find in his writings a most disturbing answer to the question: Why do bad things happen to good people? It is that there are no "good people." The puzzle should rather be why good things happen to bad people! We are good people only by the standards of bad people.

Jeremiah says that "from the least to the greatest of them, every one is greedy for unjust gain; and from prophet to priest, every one deals falsely" (Jer 6:13). Worst of all, this is covered up: "They have healed the wound of my people lightly, saying, 'Peace, peace,' when there is no peace" (Jer 6:14).

Jeremiah's fellow prophet Isaiah goes so far as to say that "we have all become like one who is unclean, and all our righteous deeds are like a polluted garment" (Is 64:6); "like filthy rags," says the King James version. Not our worst but our best, our righteousness, is filthy rags, infested with impurities. Our generosity is mixed with self-interest, our passion for justice mixed with our lust for vengeance, our love for God mixed with our fear of God. (Why else do we find it so hard to begin to pray?)

According to Jeremiah, all the prophets, and all the Bible, sin is not just a few baddies committed by goodies, bad deeds done by basically good people. Yet that is what nearly all modern psychology tells us. By biblical standards, that is nothing less than a false religion. Paul Vitz (*Psychology as Religion*) and Kirk Kilpatrick (*Psychological Seduction*) have let that cat out of the bag. Psychology has its own God: the self. But according to the Bible, the self is diseased, fallen, infected with sin as with a cancer. Sin is not just a few deeds but a chronic condition. We sin because we are sinners, just as we die because we are mortal.

C.S. Lewis in chapter four of *The Problem of Pain* has listed and refuted most of the reasons why the modern mind no longer believes in sin. I will not repeat them here, but send my readers to that classic. Lewis uses convincing experiential reasons to support what God's prophets tell us: that our question why bad things happen to good people is unanswerable because it is a false question; it is what logicians call a complex question, like "Have you stopped beating your wife?" It assumes something that is simply false, in this case that we are good people.

Oh, we are good ontologically. God didn't make junk, and we still bear his image, however defaced. That is why a single human person has a value greater than all the money or efficiency in the world, and why it is wrong to sacrifice people for things (which is the essence of war). That is also why euthanasia is wrong; people should not be sacrificed for relief from suffering.

But though ontologically we are very good, morally we are not. We are sinners. Our world is a battlefield strewn with broken treaties, broken families, broken promises, broken lives, and broken hearts. We are good stuff gone bad, a defaced masterpiece, a rebellious child. "We are not merely imperfect creatures who need to grow, we are rebels who need to lay down our arms" (C.S. Lewis).

The two essential points of Christian doctrine are sin and salvation, the disease and the cure. This is the unchangeable two-point outline of every Christian theology from Paul in Romans to Pascal in the *Pensees*. Suffering may be necessary for the cure—we may be able to cast light on why we suffer—but only if there is a disease.

Muslims have prophets too, and one of them tells this Jeremiah-like fable. A man said to Allah, "Grant me all the desires of my heart." Allah replied, "You know not what you ask. Therefore, to show you your heart, I grant your request." Immediately, the man's neighbor's house collapsed, for his neighbor was very rich and the man had always looked on his neighbor's house with envy and resentment. Rushing out to see what had happened, the man collided with a small child who was in the way. He looked angrily down at the child, and the child disappeared off the face of the earth. The man then understood, and begged Allah, "No more, please, no more!"

Are the prophets right? Dare to look into your heart. Don't

you find hate, lust, greed, and idolatry there? Do you love your enemies? Wouldn't you like to be seduced by the man or woman of your dreams? Don't you want to win a million dollars? Don't you love and long for a thousand assorted creatures more than for the creator? Be honest. Look at your heart, not your rationalizations, and judge by God's standards, not the world's. When we descend into ourselves, we emerge either as Jeremiahs or as fools. Fools call rags jewels because they judge by the ragpicker's standards.

Now how does the fact of our sin give suffering meaning? How does the darkness of sin cast light on the darkness of suffering?

In a universe created and maintained by a God powerful enough to abolish all suffering at once, loving enough to want only our blessedness, and wise enough to know always what makes for our blessedness, the only reason serious enough to justify God's continued tolerance of suffering is our need for it. "Love may cause pain to its object but only [if] that object needs alteration to become fully lovable" (C.S. Lewis). Suffering fills the need to continually remind us of the most obvious and evident truth there is, yet the one we are the most constantly forgetting in practice: that we are not God.

This implies that we are incredible fools and that left to ourselves we would play God. Blessedness leads us indeed to luxury, pride, and disaster; in short, we are all morally and spiritually insane, fractured to our very core. That core, that heart, is our relationship to God, as a character's essence is his relationship to his author, who alone holds the secret of his identity.

Thus our suffering is compatible with God's love if it is medicinal, remedial, and necessary; i.e., if we are very sick. As a certain wise teacher of old put it, "Those who are well have no need of a physician, but those who are sick. . . . I came not to call the righteous, but sinners" (Mt 9:12). Jesus as physician offers us a cure, and that is the good news. But he first tells us, as the prophets do, the bad news, the old news, that we are sick.

We have forgotten the old news; that is why we do not understand the new news. We need to hear the weeping prophet today; we need to be insulted and told that we are not good people, that "all our righteousness is as filthy rags." For we no longer think we are desperately ill today, and that is the most desperate illness of all. It is also the reason why suffering is to us a scandal. "The Gospel appeared as good news. It brought news of possible healing to men who knew that they were mortally ill. But all this has changed. Christianity now has to preach the diagnosis—in itself very bad news—before it can win a hearing for the cure" (C.S. Lewis).

Clue Five: Hosea—Suffering Is a Note in a Love Song.

Hosea wondered about suffering too, and God gave him and his people a shocking and wonderful answer. God commanded Hosea to marry a prostitute (which he did) who was continually unfaithful to him, to show Israel that she was just such an unfaithful wife to the God who loved her as a husband:

> "Plead with your mother, plead—
> for she is not my wife,
> and I am not her husband—
> that she put away her harlotry from her face,
> and her adultery from between her breasts;
> lest I strip her naked
> and make her as in the day she was born,
> and make her like a wilderness,
> and set her like a parched land,
> and slay her with thirst.
> Upon her children also I will have no pity,
> because they are children of harlotry.
> For their mother has played the harlot;

she that conceived them has acted shamefully.
For she said, 'I will go after my lovers,
who give me my bread and my water,
my wool and my flax, my oil and my drink.'" (Hos 2:2-5)

This does not sound very loving. But it is. And it is
illuminating too. The clue about suffering here is that God
uses it to win back his faithless bride to his love:

"Therefore I will hedge up her way with thorns;
and I will build a wall against her,
so that she cannot find her paths.
She shall pursue her lovers,
but not overtake them;
and she shall seek them,
but shall not find them.
Then she shall say, 'I will go
and return to my first husband,
for it was better with me then than now.'
And she did not know
that it was I who gave her
the grain, the wine, and the oil,
and who lavished upon her silver
and gold which they used for Baal." (Hos 2:6-8)

What seems at first an expression of God's wrath turns out to
be an expression of God's love:

"Therefore I will take back
my grain in its time,
and my wine in its season;
and I will take away my wool and my flax,
which were to cover her nakedness.
Now I will uncover her lewdness
in the sight of her lovers,

and no one shall rescue her out of my hand . . . .
Therefore, behold, I will allure her,
and bring her into the wilderness,
and speak tenderly to her.
And there I will give her her vineyards,
and make the Valley of Achor a door of hope.
And there she shall answer as in the days
of her youth,
as at the time when she came out of
the land of Egypt.
"And in that day, says the Lord, you will call me, 'My husband,' and no longer will you call me, 'My Baal.' For I will remove the names of the Baals from her mouth, and they shall be mentioned by name no more. And I will make for you a covenant on that day with the beasts of the field, the birds of the air, and the creeping things of the ground; and I will abolish the bow, the sword, and war from the land; and I will make you lie down in safety. And I will betroth you to me for ever; I will betroth you to me in righteousness and in justice, in steadfast love, and in mercy." (Hos 2:9-10, 14-19)

A holy woman of old, the Lady Julian of Norwich, was deeply disturbed by references in the Bible to the wrath of a God she knew only as pure love. She asked God what his wrath really was. So God showed her. And she said of the showing, "I saw no wrath but on man's part."

The love of God is no human projection, but the wrath of God is. In fact, what we call the wrath of God is really the love of God as experienced by a fool. The wrath of God is the form the love of God takes when we fight it, just as darkness is the form light takes when we turn from it and run into our own shadow. We cast the shadow of wrath; God shines steadily with love, as the sun with light. God does not change. We do.

All analogies limp. Light is too impersonal an analogy for

God. It is true that "God is light and in him is no darkness at all" (1 Jn 1:5), but it is also true that God is a person. The better analogy, the one Jesus himself preferred, is "Father." A father's love for his child often has to take the form of punishment. Love punishes. A father's punishment is not from hatred or for harm. It is from love and for good. As the writer of the letter to the Hebrews says:

> Have you forgotten the exhortation which addresses you as sons?—"My son, do not regard lightly the discipline of the Lord, nor lose courage when you are punished by him. For the Lord disciplines him whom he loves, and chastises every son whom he receives." It is for discipline that you have to endure. God is treating you as sons; for what son is there whom his father does not discipline? If you are left without discipline, in which all have participated, then you are illegitimate children and not sons. Besides this, we have had earthly fathers to discipline us and we respected them. Shall we not much more be subject to the Father of spirits and live? For they disciplined us for a short time at their pleasure, but he disciplines us for our good, that we may share his holiness. (Heb 12:5-10)

The greatest love poem ever written sees suffering in the same way as Hosea does. The bride (symbolizing Israel and the Church) in *Song of Songs* longs for union with her bridegroom (God). But the bride attains this consummation only after going through the wilderness (symbolic of suffering). Before that, she only longs for the touch of her lover: "O that his left hand were under my head and that his right hand embraced me!" (Sg 2:6). Before that, he has to convince her to come out of hiding: "Arise, my love, my fair one, and come away. O my dove, in the clefts of the rock, in the covert of the cliff, let me see your face, let me hear your voice, for your voice is sweet, and your face is comely" (Sg 2:13-14). Before that, she gives excuses for not responding immediately to his call: "I slept, but my heart was awake. Hark! My beloved is knocking. 'Open to me, my sister, my love, my dove, my perfect one; For my head is wet with dew, my locks with the drops of the night.' I had put off my garment, how could I put it on? I had bathed my feet, how could I soil them?" (Sg 5:2-3). Only after she comes from the wilderness does she (1) trust her beloved enough to lean on him, (2) actually touch him by leaning on him, and (3) consummate their love: "Who is that coming up from the wilderness, leaning upon her beloved? Under the apple tree I awakened you" (Sg 8:5).

Love is strengthened and perfected by suffering. Couples who have had only ease lack depth. True love needs to suffer. "The course of true love never did run smooth."

Kindness—mere kindness—cannot tolerate suffering. Love can.

> By the goodness of God we mean nowadays almost exclusively his lovingness; and in this we may be right. But by Love, in this context, most of us mean kindness—the desire to see others than the self happy; not happy in this way or that, but just happy. What would really satisfy us would be a God who said of anything we happened to like doing, "What does it matter so long as they are contented?" We want, in fact, not so much a Father in heaven as a grandfather in heaven—a senile benevolence who, as they say, "liked to see young people enjoying themselves" and whose plan for the universe was simply that it might be truly said at the end of each day, "a good time was had by all."

But God's wisdom is a bit deeper than "have a nice day."

> Love is something more stern and splendid than mere kindness . . . . when kindness . . . is separated from the other elements of love, it involves a certain fundamental indifference to its object, and even something like contempt of it

. . . . we have all met people whose kindness to animals is constantly leading them to kill animals lest they should suffer. (C.S. Lewis)

Clue Six: Joel—The Day of the Lord

Joel and a few other prophets speak of a great future event which they call simply "the day of the Lord." On this day, the mystery of suffering and the deeper and more original mysteries of sin and death will be solved, not just in theory but in practice; not just explained but removed. God will tie up the loose ends of the torn tapestry of history, and the story which now seems to be a tortured tangle will appear as a masterpiece of wisdom and beauty. Here are the four most important things the prophets say about the day of the Lord:

1. Since the solution is God's, it is not ours. All our attempts to solve the most basic problems of human life have failed in theory and in practice. After thousands of years we have tamed the moon but we have not tamed man. We have reached the heavens but we have not reached heaven. We have controlled nature but not our own nature. We have gained the whole world and lost our own soul. And what does that profit us?

2. Since the solution is future, it is not yet. We are in a story, and only the end of the story explains the rest of it, just as only the conclusion of an argument explains why the premises are selected as they are. The conclusion of a story is its point, as the conclusion of an argument is its point. Puzzles in the early chapters are solved only in the final chapter.

3. Since the problem is real—real people really suffer, sin, and die—therefore, the solution must be real. God must do something, not just sit there, because we did something. He must do something, not just say something, because actions speak louder than words. His word must come into history. Philosophical and even mystical solutions to the problem of evil cannot go as far as "the day of the Lord," the definitive divine deed, which Jesus does. Buddha only *sees*: Jesus *acts*.

4. Since the "day of the Lord" is God's and is in the future and is a not-yet event (rather than a human idea which would be thinkable at any time), it is therefore mysterious to us because we are not God and not yet at the end.

"The day of the Lord," of course, is the coming of Jesus. His three comings, past, present, and future, are the solution to the problem of evil. He came on Calvary, he comes in faith to hearts and lives, and he will come again into our world at the end to establish his kingdom, heaven on earth, the thing we have always obscurely longed for and fought for and failed at. That is the prophetic promise, the heavenly hope.

Clue Seven: Isaiah—Messiah, Atonement, and Resurrection

The greatest writer among the prophets is certainly Isaiah. His writing reminds me of John the Evangelist, who is symbolized in traditional Christian art as an eagle; both writers soar, and our spirits soar with them. It is fitting that the three clues that most clearly point to Jesus are from Isaiah.

First, the idea of the Messiah, or promised one. God's intervention in history, the day of the Lord, will be the work of one man. "The hopes and fears of all the years" are on his shoulders. He's the ace relief pitcher who can strike out the opposing batters even though no one else can. He's God's trump card. Who he will be and what he will be remain mysterious in Isaiah, but *that* he will be is God's solemn promise.

Second, the Messiah will make atonement, at-one-ment, reconciliation, restitution between man and God by conquering sin; between man and man by conquering war (he will be the Prince of Peace); and even between man and nature by conquering suffering. In the peaceable kingdom, the lion and lamb shall lie down together, the little child will be able to put his hand in the snake's den without fear, and no one will hurt anyone or destroy anything in all the realm.

How will he accomplish this? Somehow, by suffering

himself. "With his stripes we are healed" (Is 53:5). Reread the whole fifty-third chapter of Isaiah sometime. Why not now?

Christians understand more of this chapter than Isaiah or his contemporaries did. We know who the Redeemer is. But no one knows to this day how redemption works, any more than we know how gravity works.

Vicarious atonement, the innocent suffering for the guilty, was not a new idea in Christianity. It was in Old Testament Judaism, especially in Isaiah. Jews usually interpret Isaiah 53 as referring to the Jewish people collectively rather than to any individual. For if it does refer to an individual, Jesus is the almost inescapable candidate for the position. Though the idea of vicarious atonement seems grossly unjust, it touches a need and a nerve deeper in us than rational justice. Part of it is the need to find sense and purpose and use for what seems to be the most useless thing in our lives, the sufferings of the innocent. What good could possibly be accomplished by a great man's early death, paralysis, or insanity? What is this waste for? Not for him. It does not seem to do him any good. The notion of vicarious atonement says that it does *someone* good, that God uses even what seems like the waste of one life to fertilize another. Would we really rather have the waste wasted? Would we rather tell the hopeless paralytic that there was no purpose to his suffering, that he was now totally useless? How merciful, how compassionate is this idea that seems so unjust!

It is the Messiah, of course, who will atone for our sins. But he is no freak; he illustrates a universal principle. Therefore we too can participate somehow in vicarious atonement; our sufferings too can atone, if they are somehow one with his.

The third startling idea in Isaiah is that at some future time, presumably in the time of the Messiah, in "the day of the Lord," God will raise the dead. The most direct and simple answer to the problem of death is resurrection—an answer so simple it's hilariously funny. The resurrection is the biggest joke in history, a joke on all the philosophers, who seek to explain death, and on all the mystics, who seek to rise above it in spirit. Jesus rose above it in the body! How utterly crass, crude, and direct! The divine style is as subtle as the Big Bang. Just the thing a child would think of. God never grows up.

Death will be swallowed up in resurrection, and sin in atonement. Then suffering will cease. Once Messiah conquers sin and death, suffering will be a cinch. But it may take some time. We are in a long story, after all.

*   *   *

The clues have been inching their way forward closer and closer to a certain someone whose identity is no surprise. The story is an old one by now. Yet it is a new one too, a gospel, a good news. It is that "beauty ancient yet ever new" which we, like the whole world, have always been seeking, looking for, longing for, whether we knew it or not. The reader of this book can expect no surprise about the identity of the one to whom the clues point. It is like reading a great story for the second time: the tooth-chattering suspense is gone, but that is no regret, for it enables us to savor the story, like a thirsty man who, having glutted his ravenous thirst on the first glass of wine, is now able to savor and appreciate the second.

Clue Eight: John the Baptist—The Lamb of God

Jesus clearly said that the greatest of all the prophets was John the Baptist (Lk 7:28). John was the last of the old, for his job was to identify Jesus as the first of the new, and Jesus went on to say that the least in the new kingdom was greater than John, the greatest in the old.

The greatest prophet has as his job to decrease more and more so that the One he identified could increase more and more (Jn 3:30). The greatest one is the least one, the one who steps back most. The best window is the most transparent to the light. Therefore we do not have great writings from John the Baptist, as we have from the other prophets. No poetry, no great rhetoric, no moving prose. Just one word, really: "repent." In that word John summarizes the message of all the prophets, all the preparation for the Messiah. Repent; that is, turn. Turn around, face God instead of running away from him. Face the light, so that when the light comes to you with a face, the face of Jesus, you can meet him face-to-face.

John is the greatest prophet because he is the closest to the one whom all the prophets foretell, the one whom all the prophets are for, the one who is the answer not only to the problem of suffering but also to all the problems of human existence. John's finger points to God's definitive answer to the problem of suffering, the Lamb of God, the one who would solve the problem of suffering by suffering, who would solve the problem of death by dying, and in so doing transform the meaning of suffering and death. We are now ready to look at him. The prophets have done their job. Their pointing fingers, especially John's last and closest one, have led us beyond themselves, like clues, saying, "Look, look. Not here; there; yonder; ahead."

And now he is here.

SEVEN

The Clues Converge:
Jesus, the Tears of God

"Not only do we only know God through Jesus Christ, but we only know ourselves through Jesus Christ; we only know life and death through Jesus Christ. Apart from Jesus Christ we cannot know the meaning of our life or our death, of God or of ourselves."

Pascal

WE HAVE FINALLY COME HOME.

This is the most important chapter in this book, for it is the answer, the only adequate answer, to our problem of man's suffering and God's silence. We are finally led not to the answer but to the Answerer. As in Job, God ends his silence and speaks his word. Christ is the Word of God, the answer of God. All the words of the prophets, philosophers, and poets are echoes of this Word. In him all the clues converge, like many pointing fingers, all pointing from different directions and distances to the same one.

The answer must be someone, not just something. For the problem (suffering) is about someone (God—why does he . . . why doesn't he . . .?) rather than just something. To question God's goodness is not just an intellectual experiment. It is rebellion or tears. It is a little child with tears in its eyes looking up at Daddy and weeping, "Why?" This is not merely the philosophers' "why?" Not only does it add the emotion of tears but also it is asked in the context of relationship. It is a question put to the Father, not a question asked in a vacuum.

The hurt child needs not so much explanations as re-assurances. And that is what we get: the reassurance of the Father in the person of Jesus, "he who has seen me has seen the Father" (Jn 14:9).

The answer is not just a word but the Word; not an idea but a person. Clues are abstract, persons are concrete. Clues are signs; they signify something beyond themselves, something real. Our solution cannot be a mere idea, however true, profound, or useful, because that would be only another sign, another finger, another clue—like fingers pointing to other fingers, like having faith in faith, or hope in hope, or being in love with love. A hall of mirrors.

Besides being here, he is now. Besides being concretely real in our world, he, our answer, is also in our story, our history. Our story is also his-story. The answer is not a timeless truth but a once-for-all catastrophic event, as real as the stories in today's newspapers. God did not varnish over our sin and our suffering. He came into it, like a dentist or a surgeon, to get it all out. In fact, he became our garbage man. He touched and took away our garbage. God became a man; we touched him, we handled him. John the Evangelist begins his first letter in words that still tremble with awe at that fact:

> That which was from the beginning, which we have heard, which we have seen with our eyes, which we have looked upon and touched with our hands . . . . (1 Jn 1:1)

God's answer is simply the most incredible event in all of history. Eternity entered time. The mind of God, the word of life—timeless, eternal life—became as temporally alive, as jumpingly alive, as a lion.

We cannot help resisting the electric concreteness of this God:

Men are reluctant to pass over from the notion of an abstract and negative deity to the living God. I do not wonder. Here lies the deepest taproot of Pantheism and of the objection to traditional imagery. It was hated not, at bottom, because it pictured Him as man but because it pictured Him as king, or even as warrior. The Pantheist's God does nothing, demands nothing. He is there if you wish for Him, like a book on a shelf. He will not pursue you. There is no danger that at any time heaven and earth should flee away at His glance. If He were the truth, then we could really say that all the Christian images of kingship were a historical accident of which our religion ought to be cleansed. It is with a shock that we discover them to be indispensable. You have had a shock like that before, in connection with smaller matters—when the line pulls at your hand, when something breathes beside you in the darkness. So here; the shock comes at the precise moment when the thrill of *life* is communicated to us along the clue we have been following. It is always shocking to meet life where we thought we were alone. "Look out!" we cry, "it's *alive*." And therefore this is the very point at which so many draw back—I would have done so myself if I could—and proceed no further with Christianity. An "impersonal God"—well and good. A subjective God of beauty, truth and goodness, inside our own heads—better still. A formless life-force surging through us, a vast power which we can tap—best of all. But God Himself, alive, pulling at the other end of the cord, perhaps approaching at an infinite speed, the hunter, king, husband—that is quite another matter. There comes a moment when the children who have been playing at burglars hush suddenly: was that a *real* footstep in the hall? There comes a moment when people who have been dabbling in religion ("Man's search for God!") suddenly draw back. Supposing we really found Him? We never meant it to come to *that*! Worse still, supposing He had found us?

I hope the reader is not impatient with this long quotation. I think it is the greatest paragraph of the greatest Christian apologist of our century, C.S. Lewis, from his book *Miracles*. Only the paragraph at the end of his sermon "The Weight of Glory" rivals it.

The incarnation was the biggest shock in history. Even his own people, whom he had prepared for two thousand years for this event, could not digest it: "He came to his own home, and his own people received him not" (Jn 1:11). Even his own disciples could not understand him. It was the unthinkable, "the absolute paradox" (as Kierkegaard calls it) that the eternal God should have a beginning in time, that the maker of Mary's womb should be made in Mary's womb; that the first one became second, the independent one became dependent as a little baby, dependent for his very earthly existence—not on "the will of the flesh" but on the new Eve saying yes to the angel where the old Eve had said yes to the devil.

Even the devil did not expect this folly. That God should step right into Satan's trap, Satan's world, Satan's game, the jaws of death on the cross; that he should give Satan the opportunity to cherish forever, in dark, satanic glee, the terrible words from God to God, "My God, My God, why hast Thou forsaken Me?"—this was something "no eye has seen, nor ear heard, nor the heart of man conceived" (1 Cor 2:9). That God should take alienation away from man by inserting alienation into the very heart of God; that he should conquer evil by allowing it its supreme, unthinkable triumph, deicide, the introduction of death into the life of God, the God of life, the Immortal One; that he should destroy the power of evil by allowing it to destroy him—this is "the foolishness of God [that] is wiser than men, and the weakness of God [that] is stronger than men" (1 Cor 1:25).

Calvary is judo. The enemy's own power is used to defeat him. Satan's craftily orchestrated plot, rolled along according to plan by his agents Judas, Pilate, Herod, and Caiaphas, culminated in the death of God. And this very event, Satan's conclusion, was God's premise. Satan's end was God's means. It saved the world. Christians celebrate the greatest evil and the greatest tragedy of all time as Good Friday. In the symbolic language of Revelation, the meek little Lamb (*arnion*) defeats the great and terrible Beast (*therion*) in the last battle, the fight for the heavyweight championship of the universe, by shedding his own blood. Satan's bloody plan became the means of his own despoilment. God won Satan's captives— us—back to himself by freely dying in our place.

It is, of course, the most familiar, the most often-told story in the world. Yet it is also the strangest, and it has never lost its strangeness, its awe, and will not even in eternity, where angels tremble to gaze at things we yawn at. And however strange, it is the only key that fits the lock of our tortured lives and needs. We needed a surgeon, and he came and reached into our wounds with bloody hands. He didn't give us a placebo or a pill or good advice. He gave us himself.

He came. He entered space and time and suffering. He came, like a lover. Love seeks above all intimacy, presence, togetherness. Not happiness. "Better unhappy with her than happy without her"—that is the word of a lover. He came. That is the salient fact, the towering truth, that alone keeps us from putting a bullet through our heads. He came. Job is satisfied even though the God who came gave him absolutely no answers at all to his thousand tortured questions. He did the most important thing and he gave the most important gift: himself. It is a lover's gift. Out of our tears, our waiting, our darkness, our agonized aloneness, out of our weeping and wondering, out of our cry, "My God, my God, why hast Thou forsaken me?" he came, all the way, right into that cry.

In coming into our world he came also into our suffering. He sits beside us in the stalled car in the snowbank. Sometimes he starts the car for us, but even when he doesn't, he is there. That is the only thing that matters. Who cares about cars and success and miracles and long life when you have God sitting beside you? He sits beside us in the lowest places of our lives, like water. Are we broken? He is broken with us. Are we rejected? Do people despise us not for our evil but for our good, or attempted good? He was "despised and rejected of men." Do we weep? Is grief our familiar spirit, our horrifyingly familiar ghost? Do we ever say, "Oh, no, not again! I can't take any more!"? He was "a man of sorrows and acquainted with grief." Do people misunderstand us, turn away from us? They hid their faces from him as from an outcast, a leper. Is our love betrayed? Are our tenderest relationships broken? He too loved and was betrayed by the ones he loved. "He came unto his own and his own received him not." Does it seem sometimes as if life has passed us by or cast us out, as if we are sinking into uselessness and oblivion? He sinks with us. He too is passed over by the world. His way of suffering love is rejected, his own followers often the most guilty of all; they have made his name a scandal, especially among his own chosen people. What Jew finds the road to him free from the broken weapons of bloody prejudice? We have made it nearly impossible for his own people to love him, to see him as he is, free from the smoke of battle and holocaust.

How does he look upon us now? With continual sorrow, but never with scorn. We add to his wounds. There are nineteen hundred nails in his cross. We, his beloved and longed for and passionately desired, are constantly cold and correct and distant to him. And still he keeps brooding over the world like a hen over an egg, like a mother who has had all of her beloved children turn against her. "Could a mother desert her young? Even so I could not desert you." He sits beside us not only in our sufferings but even in our sins. He does not turn his face from us, however much we turn our face from him. He endures our spiritual scabs and scars, our sneers and screams, our hatreds and haughtiness, just to be with us. Withness—that is the word of love.

Does he descend into all our hells? Yes. In the unforgettable line of Corrie ten Boom from the depths of a Nazi death camp, "No matter how deep our darkness, he is deeper still." Does he descend into violence? Yes, by suffering it and leaving us the solution that to this day only a few brave souls have dared to try, the most notable in this century not even a Christian but a Hindu. Does he descend into insanity? Yes, into that darkness too. Even into the insanity of suicide? Can he be there too? Yes he can. "Even the darkness is not dark to him." He finds or makes light even there, in the darkness of the mind—perhaps not until the next world, until death's release.

For the darkest door of all has been shoved open and light from beyond it has streamed into our world to light our way, since he has changed the meaning of death. It is not merely that he rose from the dead, but that he changed the meaning of death, and therefore also of all the little deaths, all the sufferings that anticipate death and make up parts of it. Death, like a cancer, seeps back into life. We lose little bits of life daily—our health, our strength, our youth, our hopes, our dreams, our friends, our children, our lives—all these dribble away like water through our desperate, shaking fingers. Nothing we can do, not our best efforts, holds our lives together. The only lives that don't spring leaks are the ones that are already all watery. The only hearts that do not break are the ones that are busily constructing little hells of loveless control, cocoons of safe, respectable selfishness to insulate themselves from the tidal wave of tears that comes sooner or later.

But he came into life and death, and he still comes. He is still here. "As you did it to one of the least of these my brethren, you did it to me" (Mt 25:40). He is here. He is in us and we are in him; we are his body. He is gassed in the ovens of Auschwitz. He is sneered at in Soweto. He is cut limb from limb in a thousand safe and legal death camps for the unborn strewn throughout our world, where he is too tiny for us to see or care about. He is the most forgotten soul in the world. He is the one we love to hate. He practices what he preaches: he turns his other cheek to our slaps. That is what love is, what love does, and what love receives.

Love is why he came. It's all love. The buzzing flies around the cross, the stroke of the Roman hammer as the nails tear into his screamingly soft flesh, the infinitely harder stroke of his own people's hammering hatred, hammering at his heart—why? For love. God is love, as the sun is fire and light, and he can no more stop loving than the sun can stop shining.

Henceforth, when we feel the hammers of life beating on our heads or on our hearts, we can know—we must know—that he is here with us, taking our blows. Every tear we shed becomes his tear. He may not yet wipe them away, but he makes them his. Would we rather have our own dry eyes, or his tear-filled ones? He came. He is here. That is the salient fact. If he does not heal all our broken bones and loves and lives now, he comes into them and is broken, like bread, and we are nourished. And he shows us that we can henceforth use our very brokenness as nourishment for those we love. Since we are his body, we too are the bread that is broken for others. Our very failures help heal other lives; our very tears help wipe away tears; our being hated helps those we love. When those we love hang up on us, he keeps the lines open. His withness with us enables us to be with those who refuse to be with us.

Perhaps he is even in the sufferings of animals, if, as Scripture seems to say, we are somehow responsible for them and they suffer with us. He not only sees but suffers the fall of each sparrow.

All our sufferings are transformable into his work, our passion into his action. That is why he instituted prayer, says Pascal: to bestow on creatures the dignity of causality. We are really his body; the Church is Christ as my body is me. That is why Paul says his sufferings are making up in his own body what Christ has yet to endure in his body (Col 1:24).

Thus God's answer to the problem of suffering not only really happened 2,000 years ago, but it is still happening in our own lives. The solution to our suffering is our suffering! All our suffering can become part of his work, the greatest work ever done, the work of salvation, of helping to win for those we love eternal joy.

How? This can be done on one condition: that we believe. For faith is not just a mental choice within us; it is a transaction with him. "Behold, I stand at the door and knock; if any one ... opens the door, I will come in and eat with him" (Rev 3:20). To believe, according to John's Gospel, is to receive (Jn 1:12), to receive what God has already done. His part is finished ("It is finished," he said on the cross). Our part is to receive that work and let it work itself out in and through our lives, including our tears. We offer it up to him, and he really takes it and uses it in ways so powerful that we would be flattened with wonder if we knew them now.

You see, the Christian views suffering, as he views everything, in a totally different way, a totally different context, than the unbeliever. He sees it and everything else as a *between*, as existing between God and himself, as a gift from God, an invitation from God, a challenge from God, something between God and himself. Everything is relativized. I do not relate to an object and keep God in the background somewhere; God is the object that I relate to. Everything is between us and God. Nature is no longer just nature, but creation, God's creation. Having children is procreation. My very I is his image, not my own but on loan.

What then is suffering to the Christian? It is Christ's invitation to us to follow him. Christ goes to the cross, and we are invited to follow to the same cross. Not because it is the cross, but because it is his. Suffering is blessed not because it is suffering but because it is his. Suffering is not the context that explains the cross; the cross is the context that explains suffering. The cross gives this new meaning to suffering; it is now not only between God and me but also between Father and Son. The first *between* is taken up into the Trinitarian exchanges of the second. Christ allows us to participate in his cross because that is his means of allowing us to participate in the exchanges of the Trinity, to share in the very inner life of God.

Freud says our two absolute needs are love and work. Both are now fulfilled by our greatest fear, suffering. Work, because our suffering now becomes *opus dei,* God's work, construction work on his kingdom. Love, because our suffering now becomes the work of love, the work of redemption, saving those we love.

True love, unlike popular sentimental substitutes, is willing to suffer. Love is not "luv." Love is the cross. Our problem at first, the sheer problem of suffering, was a cross without a Christ. We must never fall into the opposite and equal trap of a Christ without a cross.

Look at a crucifix. St. Bernard of Clairvaux says that whenever he does, Christ's five wounds appear to him as lips, speaking the words, "I love you."

In summary, Jesus did three things to solve the problem of suffering. First, he came. He suffered with us. He wept. Second, in becoming man he transformed the meaning of our suffering: it is now part of his work of redemption. Our death pangs become birth pangs for heaven, not only for ourselves but also for those we love. Third, he died and rose. Dying, he paid the price for sin and opened heaven to us; rising, he transformed death from a hole into a door, from an end into a beginning.

That third thing, now—resurrection. It makes more than all the difference in the world. Many condolences begin by saying something like this: "I know nothing can bring back your dear one again, but . . ." No matter what words follow, no matter what comforting psychology follows that "but," Christianity says something to the bereaved that makes all the rest trivial, something the bereaved longs infinitely more to hear: God can and will bring back your dear one again to life. There is resurrection.

What difference does it make? Simply the difference between infinite and eternal joy and infinite and eternal joylessness. Resurrection was so important to Christ's disciples that when Paul preached the good news in Athens, the inhabitants thought he was preaching two new gods, Jesus and resurrection (*anastasis*) (Acts 17). The same Paul said, "If Christ has not been raised, then our preaching is in vain and your faith is in vain. . . . If for this life only we have hoped in Christ, we are of all men most to be pitied" (1 Cor 15:14, 19).

Because of resurrection, when all our tears are over, we will, incredibly, look back at them and laugh, not in derision but in joy. We do a little of that even now, you know. After a great worry is lifted, a great problem solved, a great sickness healed, a great pain relieved, it all looks very different as past, to the eyes of retrospection, than it looked as future, as prospect, or as present, as experience. Remember St. Teresa's bold saying that from heaven the most miserable earthly life will look like one bad night in an inconvenient hotel!

If you find that hard to believe, too good to be true, know that even the atheist Ivan Karamazov understands that hope. He says,

> I believe like a child that suffering will be healed and made up for, that all the humiliating absurdity of human contradictions will vanish like a pitiful mirage, like the despicable fabrication of the impotent and infinitely small Euclidean mind of man, that in the world's finale, at the moment of eternal harmony, something so precious will come to pass that it will suffice for all hearts, for the comforting of all resentments, for the atonement of all the crimes of humanity, of all the blood that they've shed; that it will make it not only possible to forgive but to justify all that has happened.

Why then does Ivan remain an atheist? Because though he believes, he does not accept. He is not a doubter; he is a rebel. Like his own character the Grand Inquisitor, Ivan is angry at God for not being kinder. That is the deepest source of unbelief: not the intellect but the will.

The story I have retold in this chapter is the oldest and best known of stories. For it is the primal love story, the story we most love to tell. Tolkien says, "There is no tale ever told that men would rather find was true." It is suggested in the fairy tales, and it is why we find the fairy tales so strangely compelling. Kierkegaard retells it beautifully and profoundly in chapter two of *Philosophical Fragments,* in the story of the king who loved and wooed the humble peasant maiden. It is told symbolically in the greatest of love poems, the Song of Songs, favorite book of the mystics. And the very loveliness of it is an argument for its truth. Indeed, how could this crazy idea, this crazy desire, ever have entered into the mind and heart of man? How could a creature without a digestive system learn to desire food? How could a creature without manhood desire a woman? How could a creature without a mind desire knowledge? And how could a creature with no capacity for God desire God?

Let's step back a bit. We began with the mystery, not just of suffering but of suffering in a world supposedly created by a loving God. How to get God off the hook? God's answer is Jesus. Jesus is not God off the hook but God on the hook. That's why the doctrine of the divinity of Christ is crucial: If that is not God there on the cross but only a good man, then God is not on the hook, on the cross, in our suffering. And if God is not on the hook, then God is not off the hook. How could he sit there in heaven and ignore our tears?

There is, as we saw, one good reason for not believing in God: evil. And God himself has answered this objection not in words but in deeds and in tears. Jesus is the tears of God.

EIGHT

What Difference Does It Make? Seven Lessons from the Saints, the Fingers of Jesus

"Life holds only one tragedy: not to have been a saint."
Charles Peguy

I LOVE WILLIAM JAMES, though I do not agree with his philosophy of pragmatism. He is full of wise advice. One of my favorites is that we should always ask of any idea, "What difference does it make?" If it makes no experienceable difference whether it is true or false, then we should not bother with it. The I.I.I. (Idea's Importance Index) is the difference it makes.

If all I have said so far is true, what difference does it make to us here and now? Specifically, what do we do about it? If we believe it, what next?

How do we find out? We ask those who have experienced the difference it makes, viz., the fingers of Jesus, the saints. Saints are simply people who love him most dearly, know him most clearly, and follow him most nearly. In the scriptural sense, all Christians are saints, more or less. In the popular sense, saints are the "more." The point is that Jesus is still at work in them, in his Body, his people. We see the difference he makes there. What do they say about applying the Jesus-solution to the suffering problem?

1. "I Never Promised You a Rose Garden."

For one thing, they expect suffering since Jesus has specifically told us to: he, the Christian's model, was the man of sorrows, and his best people throughout the ages have always suffered the most. "The cross is the gift God gives to his friends," says St. Philip Neri.

Because we are Christ's Body and cannot be ahead of him as our leader, trials are in the cards for us. "In the world you will have tribulation; but be of good cheer, I have overcome the world" (Jn 16:33). This world is a "vale of tears," and all our technological genius has not been able to dry our tears. If anything, the modern world is wetter within, though dryer without. (Or is it? Fifty million died in World War II, and the lives of billions totter on the brink of World War III.)

The point of our lives in this world is not comfort, security, or even happiness, but training; not fulfillment but preparation. It's a lousy home, but it's a fine gymnasium. It is an uphill bowling alley. The point is not to knock down all the pins (people who do that are usually cheating) but to train our muscles. The ball isn't supposed to reach the pins, the goal. "One step forward, one backward" is our law here. Progress is a myth. The stronger we get, the weaker we get, the more dependent on our crutches, our machines. For we misunderstand where we are if we believe in earthly utopias. The universe is a soul-making machine, a womb, an egg. Jesus didn't make it into a rose garden when he came, though he could have. Rather, he wore the thorns from this world's gardens.

If we believe that, we will expect sufferings rather than resent them as a scandal. "We have no right to happiness," said C.S. Lewis in the last article he ever wrote. Malcolm Muggeridge calls the phrase "the pursuit of happiness" in our American Declaration of Independence one of the silliest things ever said.

The point of this life is not to be happy but to become real, like the Velveteen Rabbit; to be tamed by God, as the fox says in *The Little Prince,* to become the person God can love perfectly, to satisfy his thirst to love. God doesn't want perfect performances but loving persons; he is not a stage manager but a lover. Being counts more than doing, the singer more than the song. We learn by the mistakes we make and the sufferings they bring. If we haven't made at least half a dozen mistakes today, we aren't trying hard enough. Even Jesus, according to Scripture, "learned obedience through suffering." Are we better than he is?

And the best fruit, the most beautiful flower, of suffering is forgiveness, "the plant that blossoms only when watered with tears." There is no alternative to forgiveness except hell, according to Jesus' parables. And the way we become forgiving is by suffering. The only alternative to suffering here is suffering there.

We had better stop looking for alternatives, for escape hatches, for this is our hatchery.

2. "Everything Is Grace."

St. Teresa says, simply, that everything is grace. Suffering is something. Therefore suffering too is grace.

We know what God is like. Jesus. God is infinite, eternal, pure, absolute, unqualified love. Everything he does, therefore, is love. Everything that comes to us, therefore, is his kiss. Sometimes his kiss is full of tears.

"All things work together for good to them that love God" (Rom 8:28, KJV). Romans 8:28 is, I think, the most amazing verse in Scripture. Yet its alternative is unthinkably awful. Romans 8:28 is one of two possible answers to the ultimate question, what is ultimate? Is everything light, surrounding little pockets of darkness? Or is everything darkness, surrounding little pockets of light?

Jesus shows us as well as tells us the answer. Everything is God's love, God's grace. Rabbi Kushner is wrong; bad things do not happen to good people because God is weak, or still a growing baby; nature does not surround and limit and determine the meaning and acts of God. Grace surrounds gravity, gravity does not surround grace. Our lives are not determined by the blind laws of nature's necessity, fate, or chance. Rather, nature is determined by a creator and lover, an author of a drama. Nature is only the stage set for life. Human life is not a trivial addition to nature; nature is a trivial aspect of our lives, like the props to a play. And the difference this makes is total. Everything is meaningful. In fact, everything is grace. The alternative is simply Ecclesiastes' "vanity of vanities."

We cannot know what the meaning of every event is, but we can know that every event is meaningful. How? Neither science nor philosophy can prove it or disprove it. But we have been told by God's Word (Scripture) and by God's Word (Jesus); and we also know it by experience, by the experience of loving. Love alone understands love. Only if our will is in line with the Father's will, says Jesus, will we understand him and his teaching (Jn 7:17). If we love God, we will understand that everything is grace, that Job's sores were grace, that Job's abandonment was grace, that even Jesus' abandonment ("My God, my God, why hast Thou forsaken Me?") was grace. Even the delay of grace is grace. Suffering is grace. The cross is grace. The grave is grace. Even hell is made of God's love and grace, experienced as pain by those who hate it. There is nothing but God's love. "Everything is grace."

What do we do about that?

Not a passive resignation. For our activity too is grace. Our struggle against suffering and every form of evil, physical and spiritual, is part of God's will for us and part of our growing. But at the same time as we thus say no to suffering, disease, death, and diminishments, we also say yes to God's overall plan, which includes both our efforts and their failure to fully conquer. It is like being in a play. Even as you are enacting the will of the character, you are also enacting the will of the author. Even as your character may fall, your author stands, and unless the character fights and falls, the author does not stand. For the character to refuse to fight because he knows the script, and knows that he will not win, is for him to fight against the author. Resignation to God but nonresignation to the world, not fighting God but fighting the evils of the world—that is our destiny.

3. *"Fiat"*

Mary's single word is all we need to know. All the secret of sanctity is here: "Be it done to me according to Thy word." For "Thy word" has been revealed as Jesus.

What difference does Jesus make to *fiat?*

We can do this, we can turn the skeleton key to sanctity, only because we can totally trust the God we say *fiat* to; and we can totally trust him only because we know he loves us; and we know he loves us only because of Jesus. Pascal says: "Not only do we only know God through Jesus Christ, but we only know ourselves through Jesus Christ; we only know life and death through Jesus Christ. Apart from Jesus Christ we cannot know the meaning of our life or our death, of God or of ourselves." The apostle Paul says: "All things were created through him and for him. He is before all things, and in him all things hold together" (Col 1:16-17).

Remove Jesus and the knowledge of God becomes questionable. If the knowledge of God is questionable, trusting this unknown God becomes questionable. And then our *fiat* becomes questionable. Jesus alone makes the secret of sanctity psychologically possible. Suffering is the obstacle. Suffering is the evidence against God, the reason not to trust him. Jesus is the evidence for God, the reason to trust him.

And the result of trust, of resting in his will, is peace. "In his will, our peace"—T.S. Eliot calls this line from Dante the profoundest in all human literature. No happiness on earth can be deeper than the happiness that comes from our willing and active submission to God's will even when he wills suffering.

And we can know that from experience.

Many things that I say, I know by faith, not by experience. But what I say now, I know both by faith and by experience, in fact by experiment, by repeated testing, by constant repetition, thousands upon thousands of times with not one exception.

Here is the result of my experiment. I know the way to perfect joy to calm energy and peaceful alertness, to never-ending and never-boring meaning and purpose, to creative inspiration, to peace of mind and satisfaction. This is not saying too much but too little. All this is how I must describe the real state of mind I have fitfully but really experienced. I know what this state is clearly, though I have experienced it only fitfully, because I have experienced it in contrast to another state, my habitual state, which is its opposite: dullness and dreariness and vague emptiness, or else frustration and unhappiness, expressed or repressed.

The way to perfect joy is incredibly simple. It is simply to die—to die to self-will and self-regard—to say to God, "Thy will be done," and mean it. To put God first, to consecrate everything—*everything*—to him.

It is not a new or original discovery. It is the basic thing all the saints say. I know it without doubt not because I have succeeded in it but because I have failed miserably at it, but know it I do, without doubt, from personal experience. If you, dear reader, do not know this too, then you must either trust me and believe it by faith, or else—much better—make for yourself the same experiment. You will, I guarantee, get the same results. And how can you afford not to try? At stake is something greater than the world.

What now follows is theory. But it is based on this fact.

Here is how *fiat,* "thy will be done," transforms suffering. To die to self and what self wants is the essence of suffering. If I want *x* and I get *y* instead, I suffer, both because I do not get *x*, which I want, and also because I get *y*, which I do not want. But if I want only God's will, I do not suffer, because I always get God's will. We suffer to the extent that we are out of line with reality, ultimate reality, God's will. Thus, paradoxically, the essence of suffering (death to self-will) can become its opposite (perfect joy) when it is undertaken freely for love of God. God not only compensates us for suffering, he turns suffering itself into perfect joy if only we obey his first and greatest commandment wholeheartedly, if we only love and will and worship him alone and above all.

Of course none of us ever do that perfectly and whole-heartedly. We are fallen, fractured creatures. And most of us, like myself, do not come even close to the degree to which the great saints do it. But even miserable specimens of humanity can do a little of it. There's a little good in the worst of us and a little bad in the best of us.

Let's go through this again. For it is only the most important practical lesson in living that I know.

Buddha saw that suffering is created by selfish desire (*tanha*). If there were no gap between what we desire and what we get, there would be no suffering. Suffering is that gap. Most people try to close the gap by getting more of what they want. It never works. Buddha tells us to close the gap by desiring less—in fact, by desiring nothing—and that this will lead us to Nirvana, the cessation or extinction of suffering through the cessation of its cause, desire.

The saints give us a third road, neither the popular road of trying to get what we desire and leaving our desires in their ordinary condition, nor Buddha's road of trying to extinguish all our desires and leaving our world in its ordinary condition, but changing our desires and thereby changing our world, wanting in a new way. First, wanting another's (God's) will instead of our own and second, consolidating our investments in desire by wanting only one thing. ("Purity of heart is to will one thing," says Kierkegaard.) Unlike Buddha's will-less and passive program, this is passionate and willful. But it is unselfish instead of selfish willing. It is a kind of willing, a kind of desire, that Buddha never dreamed of.

And—the practical point here—it leads to perfect joy. Paradoxically, the thing that leads to perfect joy is the essence of suffering: "not my will." The core of suffering, death to self-will, can lead to perfect joy, when it is freely offered to God.

Offered to God—what does that mean? Three things: faith and hope and love. These are the three catalysts that turn suffering into joy.

Jesus did it.

4. Humility and Gratitude

If we believe suffering is the touch of God's grace, we will avoid resentment, arrogance, and above all pride, the primal and satanic sin. When we suffer, our natural instinct is to resent and resist. This implies a claim to perfect happiness: how dare this suffering intrude on my self-sufficiency and control? How dare bad things happen to good people? I am good people and I deserve good things. The foregoing is precisely the attitude nearly all modern psychology explicitly teaches and popular media and advertising implicitly fosters. The alternative seems to most people to be weakness instead of meekness, something spineless and inhuman.

It is a lie. The saints are not spineless and inhuman. They are humble. Humility therefore is not spineless and inhuman.

The saints look at their lives, half full of joys and half full of sorrows, as half *full,* while others look at them as half *empty.* They know that their very existence is pure gift, by creation, and they therefore appreciate their moderate worldly joys more than the jaded worldling appreciates his millions. They know that great and joyful and neglected virtue of gratitude. No one can understand life if he is ungrateful for it. No one can totally misunderstand life if he is grateful.

What have we got to be thankful for? God, given to us eternally, that's all. Infinite joy, heaven, purchased by Jesus at an infinite cost, that's all. No, that's not all. Earth thrown in too. And self. To whom was the gift of self given at our conception? To no one, to nothing; we are pure gift. Because it is the nature of God to give. God is gift. The Trinity is an eternal self-giving and a correlative eternal gratitude. Gratitude is rooted in ultimate reality. Gift of self and gratitude for it: this is the plot of the drama of life which begins in God's eternity, is incarnated in Christ and his sacrificial death, and which presents itself as opportunity now to us. Suffering adds to this opportunity rather than takes away from it.

It is an easily verified fact, both from observation of others and from experiment yourself, that an attitude of humility and gratitude in suffering brings deep joy, while an attitude of pride and ingratitude, even without suffering, brings joylessness. Proud people simply are not happy.

Jesus made the difference here. Can you even consider Aristotle's reasonable human philosophy that makes a virtue of "proper pride" if you see the eternal Deity humbled at your feet, washing your dirt with his tears?

5. Faith

Jesus came, but he was not recognized by all because he demanded faith. Instead of the spectacular visible triumph people expected, he showed himself only to those whose hearts (not just minds and eyes) were on the lookout for him.

It is the same today. Jesus' solution to the problem of suffering is available only to faith. Use that key and you enter an incredible new world of joy and meaning; rely only on reason or feeling or sight and you will not enter.

Faith is not in feeling, but in fact. But faith results in a new feeling of joy. We can experience some of the joy of heaven now even in our suffering, as the saints did, if our faith is not pinned to feeling but only to him. "If you believe, you will see," he promises Martha at the graveside of Lazarus. Joy follows faith. For joy is not at its core a feeling at all, but a fact. Christ is our joy. He does not merely give us joy. Joy is not a feeling in us. Joy does not enter into us. We enter into joy: "Enter into the joy of your Lord" (Mt 25:21).

We are in heaven already, in one very real sense. For heaven is not first of all a place but a person. Heaven is where Christ is. He makes heaven heaven; heaven does not make him him. And we are in Christ now (unless we are heading for hell; there is no third possibility, unless the whole message of Christ is a lie). We do not see or appreciate or experience much of heaven now; and there is much, much more to come. (How cruel to tell someone they are in full heaven now—is this all there is?) We are like unborn babies: they are in the womb that is already in the world, but they don't see that until after they're born and no longer in the womb. When we die, we are born out of this little womb called the universe. But we're there in the bigger world right now, as Emily in *Our Town* signs her address:

Grovers Corners
New Hampshire
United States of America
Western Hemisphere
Planet Earth
Solar System
The Universe
Mind of God

Mind of God = heaven, and heaven = joy. If we believe we are there, even suffering becomes part of joy. It is not felt as joy, of course. That is where faith comes in.

Is this asking too much? Consider the alternative. Without faith, where are we? "Lost in a haunted wood." Crawling along the surface of some thirty-second rate celestial slag heap. Without faith, we are not in the mind of God, i.e., not in heaven. And I think everyone knows what the alternative to heaven is. It is not earth. Earth is just the way station.

6. *Weakness Makes Strength*

The most oft-repeated teaching of Jesus is the paradox that the poor are rich, the weak are strong, the lowly are exalted. It is the point of the Beatitudes, of the Sermon on the Mount, of most of his parables; it is illustrated by his whole life, by the incarnation, the *kenosis,* the emptying. He "emptied himself, taking the form of a servant, being born in the likeness of men. And being found in human form he humbled himself and became obedient unto death, even death on a cross" (Phil 2:7-8).

This is the radical counter to the wisdom of our age, of any age. The fundamental dictum of nearly all modern psychologists is to love ourselves, to accept ourselves as we are, to feel good about ourselves. When we obey this wisdom of the world, God has two choices. He can either let us stay in that state and run the risk of becoming contented, respectable, self-righteous Pharisees; or else he can mercifully slap us out of it with a dose of suffering, frustration, and discontent with ourselves, and thus move us on to a new state. Let us call it stage two. Suffering births us into stage two, like a mother. Let us be grateful to our mothers.

In stage two we hate ourselves, i.e., we reject self-will, we turn away from self. Nearly all modern psychologists say this is the origin of all that is wrong. Jesus says it is the origin of salvation:

If any one comes to me and does not hate his own father and mother and wife and children and brothers and sisters, yes, and even his own life, he cannot be my disciple. (Lk 14:26)

To hate here does not mean to despise but to turn away from, reject, and put second.

Only when we are dissatisfied, only when we are weak, only when we are failures in ourselves, can God come in. Our failure is our success. Death is the supreme failure, the supreme weakness. And it is also God's supreme opportunity and our supreme success, our entrance into heaven and God's entrance into our deepest selves. Teilhard de Chardin sees this in *The Divine Milieu*:

> We can set no limits to the tearing up of roots that is involved on our journey into God.... There is a further step to take: the one that makes us lose all foothold within ourselves. . . . What will be the agent of that definitive transformation? Nothing less than death. . . . God must, in some way or other, make room for himself, hollowing us out and emptying us, if he is finally to penetrate into us. And in order to assimilate us in him, he must break the molecules of our being so as to re-cast and re-model us. The function of death is to provide the necessary entrance into our inmost selves.

7. The Ultimate Theology of Suffering: In the Trinity

Have you ever noticed how close joy is to tears? How when the joy is so overflowing that all other expressions are inadequate, we turn to tears? Have you ever wondered why?

Have you ever noticed that there is a kind of suffering and a kind of dying that we secretly long for, that is indescribably delicious in a mystical way? This is not ordinary suffering (unless we are masochists). But we want to die when we have a mystical experience. I felt it only twice: once when swimming in the ocean in a great storm, and once when first hearing Beethoven's Ninth Symphony. The French call sexual intercourse *le petit mal,* the little death. It is an end, a consummation, like death, yet a consummation devoutly to be wished. The mystics speak of their deep desire to die in God, to become nothing in God, everything and nothing, *todo y nada* (St. John of the Cross).

What does it mean that we long to die, to suffer total self-loss? And what does it mean that joy is close to tears, that the most wonderful things are not sweet but bittersweet? And what does Jesus have to do with it?

Here is a possible answer from the saints. It is high and palmy stuff, and I am way out of my depth in telling you about it. But I think it is true, and I found it in great minds and great writers, like C.S. Lewis, and great saints and great lovers of God, like St. John of the Cross. So I serve up a small sample to you. If it is true, it is the ultimate reason why we suffer. It locates the source of suffering, or at least the model for it, its prime analogate, as high up as you can go: in the very eternal and necessary nature of the Holy Trinity.

The saints speak of our ultimate destiny and joy as "the spiritual marriage." In marriage the two become one. In the spiritual marriage we share God's very life. What is that life? The God we get married to is a Trinity of persons each of whom eternally empties himself, dies to self. Father loves Son, not self; Son loves Father, not self; Spirit is that love between them. Spirit reveals Son, not self. Son reveals Father, not self. Father begets Son, not self. Father and Son process Spirit, not themselves. Each one dies to self eternally. This is at least akin to suffering (rather, suffering is akin to it).

> It is in this sense that . . . there may be something not all unlike pains in heaven (God grant us soon to taste them). For in self-giving, if anywhere, we touch a rhythm not only of all creation but of all being. For the Eternal Word also gives Himself in sacrifice; and that not only on Calvary.

From the highest to the lowest, self exists to be abdicated and, by that abdication, becomes the more truly self, to be thereupon yet the more abdicated, and so forever. This is not a heavenly law which we can escape by remaining earthly, nor an earthly law which we can escape by being saved. What is outside the system of self-giving is not earth, nor nature, nor "ordinary life," but simply and solely Hell. (C.S. Lewis)

NINE

Back to the Problem

"Doubts are the ants in the pants that keep faith moving."
Frederick Beuchner

Reader: Ahem!

Author: Why, hello there. We haven't heard from you in quite a while. Still awake?

Reader: I didn't fall asleep, I assure you. I was just waiting and watching you finish painting your whole word-picture before I talked back.

Author: Thank you for listening. And for talking back too. Those are two great arts, you know.

Reader: Yes. And now it's your turn to listen and mine to speak. I still have a few little questions . . .

Author: Good! I welcome them. I would have liked to hear them sooner.

Reader: I waited because I prefer to respond to your picture as a whole rather than carp at little bits and pieces of it as you're painting it. Now that you seem to be finished, I can shoot at your whole picture. I have quite a few separate shots, but each of them hits a hole in the whole, and spoils your whole picture, just as a bullet anywhere in the Mona Lisa would spoil the whole thing. Because it is a whole. It all hangs together, like a picture.

Author: Yes, it does. Or like a hanged man, a crucified man.

He's the whole, or the center of the whole. You have to hit him, you know. And that's hard to do. Because he's already let himself be hit, with the real problem, actual suffering, not just intellectual objections. But what's your gripe against him?

Reader: I have no gripe against him. But . . .

Author: Then my picture is intact. He's my answer. Look at him.

Reader: Do you mean to just ignore my questions?

Author: Certainly not. You're welcome to ask them, and I'm ready to try to answer. God doesn't want us to stop thinking. And in any case, we just can't. I'll try to answer your objections in their own terms. But if your objection is something like, "That's all very well on paper, but . . ." then I have to give a more fundamental answer.

Reader: I was going to say that. That was my first objection. What's your more fundamental answer?

Author: That my answer is not on paper but on wood.

Reader: Him again, you mean? The cross?

Author: Yes. You see, it's not that he gives the answer to suffering; he is the answer. It's not that I tried to lead you from the problem to the solution by philosophical reasoning, cleverly answering objections and building up a consistent and attractive picture. I'm not selling my picture. I'm testifying about him. I tried to lead you from the problem, via the clues, to him. He doesn't lead us to clues; they lead to him. He's God's answer to sin and death and suffering.

Reader: That's another thing. I asked for only one problem and you solve three.

Author: Don't look a gift horse in the mouth. I had to do that, because suffering is a little death and death is the consequence of sin, so we have to see suffering in terms of death and death in terms of sin. Death is a bigger problem than suffering and sin is a bigger problem than death.

Reader: Why do you say we have to see suffering in terms of death instead of death in terms of suffering?

Author: Most people see death only as pain, as a particular suffering, not as objective loss, as the scandal of the disposal of the indisposable, the dispensing of the indispensible: a person, with intrinsic value.

Reader: And what about the relation between death and sin?

Author: Most people see sin in terms of death, as if the only sin is murder and the worst sin is war, instead of seeing death in terms of sin, as the consequence of sin.

Reader: You should write a book about the bigger problems, then.

Author: I did. One about death, called *Love Is Stronger Than Death,* and one about sin and virtue, called *For Heaven's Sake,* but let's get back to him instead. He answers your first objection, "That's all very well on paper, or in theory, but ...," doesn't he? Not by what he says but by what he is and does?

Reader: Yes, I see that. But I still have objections to what you say.

Author: Fine. Let's hear them.

Reader: Here's one from your own friends: what Teresa of Avila said when she fell into the mud puddle. What did God say?—"That's how I treat all my friends." And Teresa replied, "Then it is not surprising that you have so few." I like that. A saint with spunk.

Author: All the saints have spunk, by the way, not just Teresa. Without a spine she couldn't be a woman, and if she wasn't a woman she couldn't be a saint. But what's your objection?

Reader: That that God is not good. If we treated our friends the way God treats us, we wouldn't be good. Would you call a father good if he let his kid get killed by a truck when he could have run out into the street and saved him? Of course not. Yet that's what God does to us. He could prevent all sorts of bad things from happening by intervening, but he doesn't. That doesn't sound like anything I can recognize as good. I don't want him to take away our free will, just a little more of our garbage, a little faster.

Author: That's a very old problem, and it has a very old answer. The answer is called analogy. God's goodness is different from ours, because God isn't one of us. God does things that an earthly father doesn't do because God isn't an earthly father. Goodness is not what logicians call a univocal term when applied to God and us: it's not wholly the same. But . . .

Reader: So I'm right. If a man did what God did, we wouldn't call him good.

Author: No, but if a God did it, we would. God is omniscient and knows perfectly what's best for us in the long run. He has the right to say to us: You need to suffer now. We don't have that knowledge or that right most of the time. It would be arrogant for us to say that because it would be pretending to be omniscient.

Reader: So goodness isn't univocal.

Author: No, but it's not equivocal either, but analogical. Equivocal terms have two wholly different meanings. Univocal terms have only one meaning. Analogical terms have two meanings that are partly the same and partly different. Like the goodness of a dog and the goodness of a man—they're different, but not wholly different. "Good doggy" means the dog has some qualities that we call good in a man too: loyalty and affection, for instance. But the man also has qualities the dog can't have. God is to us something like what we are to a dog.

Reader: How does this apply to suffering now?

Author: A hunter sometimes makes his dog suffer—for instance when the dog is caught in a trap, the hunter has to push the dog further into the trap, to lessen the tension on it, before he can get him out. That hurts, and if the dog were a theologian it would probably question the dogma of the goodness of man, because it can't understand what we can: the mechanism of a trap requires this push further in that causes such pain because this is the way out. God does the same to us sometimes, and we can't understand why he does it any more than the dog can understand us.

Reader: We're stuck, then.

Author: No, we can trust him, as the dog can trust its master.

Reader: What difference does it make?

Author: If we trust, we won't scream and pull and rebel and make it harder to get out.

Reader: I don't know. It's a nice analogy, but . . .

Author: But?

Reader: I don't know. Just because it's consistent doesn't mean it's true.

Author: That's right. But it does answer your objection, doesn't it?

Reader: I guess so. But here's another. Why doesn't God's policy of letting us suffer work? If God allows suffering for our good, as you say, why does it sometimes work for our bad? The concentration camps, for instance. Sure, some of the prisoners became saints, but many more became animals or corpses. Some became living corpses, worn out and empty even after they were released. Why would God allow a painful operation if he knew it wasn't going to be successful?

Author: How do you know it wasn't successful? Do you see final ends? Do you see deepest hearts?

Reader: Are you saying suffering does always work?

Author: Are you saying you know it doesn't?

Reader: I don't know. You're the one with the answers. How do you know it does?

Author: I believe it does because a good God wouldn't do anything for no reason. I believe all suffering is at least potential good, an opportunity for good. It's up to our free choice to actualize that potentiality. Not all of us benefit from suffering, learn from it, because that's up to us, up to free will. Two prisoners in the same concentration camp with the same sufferings turn out very differently, just as two identical twins often turn out very differently, because of free will.

Reader: But does God foresee the free choices we'll make?

Author: Of course. He knows everything.

Reader: Then here's another objection: the old ogre of fatalism, "the will of Allah." Suffering is the will of God, accept it—that sounds fatalistic to me. I was quite convinced by Rabbi Kushner's attack on that traditional fatalistic religious attitude of accepting evil as God's will.

Author: So was I. I thought that chapter was his best one. I'm not a fatalist.

Reader: But you believe suffering is God's will.

Author: Yes, but we're free to take different attitudes toward it. There are three philosophies of life. One is fatalism: whatever will be, will be, so accept whatever comes as God's will and don't fight it. I think that's just plain silly. Of course we're to fight evil, all kinds of evil, including the physical evil of suffering. The second philosophy of life is simply that there is no fate and we forge our own destiny alone. In that case, we have to conquer suffering or we are failures. If we believe that, we'll always feel like failures. Death will always have the last word.

Reader: What's the third philosophy? The first one is yes and the second one is no to fate. How can there be a third?

Author: The first believes in predestination or providence and not free will. The second believes in free will but not predestination or providence. The third believes in both. The third is the viewpoint of Scripture and the great Christian philosophers like Augustine and Aquinas. That's why we have to both trust and fight. It's cooperation, like love or marriage or a dance.

Reader: How can our lives be both free and foreseen by God?

Author: Our free choices are what God foresees. God's authorship authors really free characters. That's the kind of story he writes—not a story about puppets or machines or animals. It's his plan, his authorship, his predestination that makes us free. (Actually, I don't like the word predestination because of the "pre": it seems to imply that God is in time, foreseeing the future, instead of contemporary to it. He sees, not foresees, everything, all at once.)

Reader: I don't think I understand that. But let it pass. Here's another related objection. If God sees or foresees everything, why didn't he create us in heavenly bliss from the beginning instead of making us get there the hard way?

Author: Don't you remember our two fairy tales? You agreed with God's choice to make a crazy world, an interesting story, with drama and mystery and monsters.

Reader: Well, then, why couldn't he have created only the people he foresaw would be happy and go to heaven? If there's a hell, that's eternal suffering, and that's the biggest scandal of all.

Author: We should talk more about heaven and hell some other time. But to answer your question right now, once he made us free, the choice between heaven and hell is really up to us. The only way he could guarantee that everybody made it to heaven would be to make the choice for us, to take away our power to choose hell, our free will.

Reader: Well what about this world then? Couldn't God have cut down on the suffering a little? This certainly doesn't seem to be the best of all possible worlds.

Author: It isn't. That's because God gave us some of the responsibility for it, and we messed it up. He did his part perfectly; we didn't. There are all sorts of better possibilities for our world. Of course this isn't the best of all possible worlds. But that's not his fault. The only way to guarantee a world without evil is to create us unfree. Would that be a better world, do you think?

Reader: No.

Author: Do the experiment I suggested sometime. Imagine you're God. Now make a better world, do a better job, in your imagination. But you have to think through all the consequences of your improvements. Every time you prevent evil by force you remove a little more freedom. To prevent all evil, you must remove all freedom. Then there's no free good either.

Reader: Sometimes I'm not sure whether that wouldn't be better after all.

Author: For an engineer, maybe. But not for a father.

Reader: Your God has dangerous tastes.

Author: Yes. Love is the most dangerous thing in the world. The ultimate risk.

Reader: I see your picture, and I must admit it's attractive, much more than the picture of the engineer God. But I still have more objections.

Author: Fine. But—correct me if I'm wrong, but I seem to detect a different tone. As if you now half hope you'll lose the argument instead of winning it, as if you hope my God is "the God who is there."

Reader: If that were true, do you think I'd admit it?

Author: Yes, if you want to win the truth more than you want to win the argument. Now what's your next objection?

Reader: Well, I was about to say your God is too much of a perfectionist, and that I preferred a compassionate God to one who would allow small children to be tortured, even for the sake of preserving free will. I was going to quote Ivan Karamazov again, about it not being worth it . . .

Author: You were about to say that, but you changed your mind?

Reader: I think I know what you'd say in reply.

Author: What?

Reader: First, that you can't pick a God as you can pick a watermelon, or a car, or a hat—by what you prefer. The question is, what's real? Who's there? And second, that the reason God is such a perfectionist, so demanding, is that he's love, and love is more than kindness, more than compassion.

Author: I couldn't have put it better myself. Do you want to answer the rest of your objections yourself too?

Reader: I don't have any more, but if you think I'm on the brink of agreeing with you now, you're wrong. Because I can't agree with you, even if you answer all my objections and even if a part of me wants to agree with you very much.

Author: Why not? Now we come to your real reason, I think. None of these last objections was your real reason, your real motive, your real obstacle, was it? They were excuses, weren't they?

Reader: Yes. Honest excuses, though, honest questions. And since you value honesty so much, I'll be completely honest with you and tell you my real reason.

Author: Thank you. Go ahead.

Reader: I'm sorry, but your whole thing just doesn't work for me. It isn't enough. Maybe there aren't any holes in it that can't be plugged, maybe you've answered all my objections, but your story still isn't enough. I still just can't believe it, can't accept it, can't say yes to a God who lets my son or daughter die, or wife or husband leave, or friend commit suicide. You're like Job's three friends. Your words make sense, they hold together, but they just don't do it for me.

Author: Do you think any words can?

Reader: No.

Author: I agree with what I think you're saying. What do you mean by that "no"? What is it that no words can do?

Reader: Reconcile me to God. I have to hate and resent God, or somebody, for this terrible thing that you call God's drama, God's story, God's plan. If it is God's plan, I just can't help hating him. It's either that or hating myself or other people— someone, someone has to be to blame. I have to hate someone.

Author: Do you?

Reader: Yes!

Author: No!

Reader: Yes, I tell you! How can I smile when I feel like screaming?

Author: You can't. But you don't have to hate someone.

Reader: How can I pray when I feel like screaming?

Author: Can you cry?

Reader: Yes.

Author: Then begin by crying instead of screaming.

Reader: I can do that.

Author: I'm not telling you to pretend, to fake anything, to be dishonest. Suffering often makes us dishonest, you know. The fear of suffering makes us say and do and believe things we think will free us from hurt, when we think honesty and facing facts would hurt. That's a very useful lesson the psychologists teach us about ourselves. Read Scott Peck's *The Road Less Travelled*, for instance.

Reader: So what do you say I'm supposed to do, just cry?

Author: No, but begin there. Because that's honesty, that's how you really are.

Reader: Then what?

Author: Then wait.

Reader: Cry and wait? Is that all? Wait for what?

Author: For God to come and wipe your tears and melt your hardness. I can't do that. You can't even do it. But God can.

Reader: But will he?

Author: I know he will.

Reader: How? How do you know that?

Author: Because you're searching for him .

Reader: I don't even know if I believe in him.

Author: But you're searching for truth. Otherwise you wouldn't be here listening and talking back.

Reader: That's true.

Author: And God is truth. So you're searching for God, whether you know it or not. And Jesus promised that all who seek, find. And if he's God, he can't lie. So therefore you will find him. He'll come, even through the mist, through the fog, like the light from a lighthouse. You'll see him through your tears. That's a promise.

Reader: Hmmm. That promise makes it like a scientific experiment: if you're right, I will find him, and if you're wrong, I won't.

Author: Yes. It's just a matter of two things: seeking and waiting.

Reader: You said cry and wait.

Author: For you, crying is a way of seeking him. Even when you hate him.

Reader: I don't understand that. How is hating God seeking God?

Author: Hate is infinitely closer to love than indifference. God makes saints out of rebels, lovers out of haters: Paul, Augustine, Ignatius. But not out of indifference. That's one of the reasons he allows you to suffer: to bring you to him, by whatever road. Tears are not indifference, and indifference is the only road that never gets to God.

Reader: He sounds pretty selfish: to let me suffer just so that he can get me.

Author: Oh, no. It's just the opposite: so you can get him. It's for your sake, not his. He's the joy you've always wanted, in and through everything you've ever wanted. Now your tears are your road to him even while you think they're your reason for turning away from him. You can't escape. Not even into tears. He was there too.

Reader: You're making me feel very uncomfortable.

Author: I don't mean to do that, but I think your heart and mind are both split: half wants to accept God and his plan for you, even including suffering, and trust to him that it's really out of love and for your good, and the other half doesn't. Isn't that true?

Reader: Maybe.

Author: Only God can win your heart. But I can help win your mind maybe. I think that's split too, isn't it?

Reader: Yes. Even though you answered my objections, something is still missing. Rationally, your case seems tight, but there's something else . . . I don't mean feeling or even will. That's another thing, my free will's choice. I mean something else in the mind. Seeing, I guess you'd call it. I think I just don't see things as you do.

Author: I think you're right. And I think I know why.

Reader: Why?

Author: Because your mind is typically modern. You're a child of your time. And the modern mind has some key difficulties understanding, seeing the Christian vision of things, especially as it applies to suffering.

Reader: What difficulties?

Author: I think we should explore that question next. They're your last intellectual obstacle. As for your free choice, that's another thing.

TEN

Why Modernity Can't Understand Suffering

"Paganism was the biggest thing in the world, and Christianity was bigger, and everything else has been comparatively small."
                                        G.K. Chesterton

As THE DIALOG IN THE LAST CHAPTER DISCOVERED, there are two obstacles to belief in the Christian answer to the problem of suffering: intellectual and volitional obstacles. Words can help overcome the intellectual, but grace and free choice are both needed to overcome the volitional ones.

The intellectual obstacles are of two kinds. The previous chapter dealt with the rational obstacles, the logical objections. This chapter deals with the deeper intellectual obstacle, the things that the modern mind does not see, the big things that have dropped out of its narrowed vision.

We are all part of modernity. Even if we criticize it, we are influenced by it. It is like the family you grew up in; even if you leave it, it remains a part of you. There are at least seven things which the modern mind forgets and therefore which modern Christians have to fight to preserve; these seven things are the necessary background for the Christian vision's answer to the problem of suffering. They are also crucial for other reasons, among them the survival of civilization and sanity. But we speak of them here only in relation to our problem, suffering.

1. *Modernity's New* Summum Bonum

Around the time of the Renaissance, the Western mind began to formulate a new idea, a new answer to this question: What is the best thing in life? What is the point, purpose, meaning, goal, or good of living? What is the *summum bonum,* or greatest good?

Different societies have given different answers to this most important of all questions. But all ancient answers had one thing in common, and that one thing was denied by the new answer of modernity, by post-Renaissance, Western, pluralistic, humanistic, secular, democratic, technological society. No one has put the difference more succinctly than C. S. Lewis in *The Abolition of Man:*

> For the wise men of old, the cardinal problem of human life was how to conform the soul to objective reality, and the solution was wisdom, self-discipline, and virtue. For the modern mind, the cardinal problem is how to subdue reality to the wishes of man, and the solution is a technique.

To the premodern mind, "objective reality" meant God, or gods of some sort; the same term connotes to the modern mind first of all the physical universe. It is silly to try to subdue reality if reality is God; but it is also silly to conform to it if it means only rocks and rainbows.

Francis Bacon trumpeted the new era in his slogan "knowledge for power." The old idea that knowledge was for truth or virtue, the contemplative and moral ideal, was to be replaced by a more practical, efficient, take charge attitude. Truth was a means, not an end. The new end was power, or man's conquest of nature.

In *The Abolition of Man,* one of the most important books of the twentieth century, Lewis brilliantly shows the joker in the pack of this new ideal. He shows that man's conquest of nature must always be some men's conquest of other men using nature as an instrument; and that if the conquerors, or controllers, or conditioners—the intelligentsia of our age— step out of the *tao*, the objective moral law, as the enormous majority have done, then they will be controlled not by supernatural ideals but by the natural forces of their own heredity and environment which happen to have determined their prejudices. Thus man's conquest of nature turns out to be nature's conquest of man.

For our purposes the relevant point of Lewis's argument is that this new ideal of human power over nature means that suffering is a scandal, a problem to be conquered rather than a mystery to be understood and a moral challenge to be lived. The conquest of suffering is what is really meant by the conquest of nature. Thus suffering becomes for modernity what it never was for any premodern civilization: the greatest problem there is, the thing that must be overcome. The greater evil of sin is seen in terms of the lesser evil of suffering. The only sin the modern mind really feels a rightful horror about is cruelty. Modernity finds it very hard to comprehend the biblical (and universal) myth of paradise lost, where suffering and death are seen in terms of sin rather than vice versa. The Christian story therefore also seems incomplete and a failure to the modern mind, for Christ conquered sin, but he did not yet abolish the need for us to suffer and die. A God who did not abolish suffering—worse, a God who abolished sin precisely by suffering—is a scandal to the modern mind, for to that mind such a solution seems to ignore the primary problem. To the Christian mind, it is modernity which ignores the primary problem.

In short, if the most important thing in life is reconciliation with God, union with God, conformity to God, then any price is worth paying to attain that end, if necessary. (Why it should be necessary to pay such a horrendous price is another question, which we shall look at in the section of this chapter about justice.) But if the most important thing in life is conquering suffering and attaining pleasure, comfort, and power by man's conquest of nature, then Jesus is a fool and a failure.

When a civilization or an individual puts a second thing, like pleasure or power, first, and makes it an obsession, an addiction, this blinds the mind's eye to understanding it. The alcoholic does not understand the true good and purpose of wine, "to gladden the heart of man." The lecher does not understand the purpose of sex, with its glorious and mystical unification of pleasure, procreation, and personal love. And the society that makes the relief of suffering its *summum bonum* does not understand the meaning of suffering or of pleasure.

2. Modernity's Loss of Faith in Ultimate Meaning

"If life as a whole has meaning, then suffering has meaning, for suffering is an inherent part of life." So wrote a modern wise man in a Nazi concentration camp. A corollary of this principle is that if life as a whole is meaningless, then suffering too is meaningless, since suffering is an inherent part of life. And to the typically modern mind, the secular mind, life as a whole is meaningless, though the parts may be meaningful. For the secular mind discounts supernatural meanings, transcendental meanings, God-made meanings, and is left only with man-made meanings. These are enough for us, it thinks. But it thinks askew. For man-made meanings are the meanings we put into the things we do or invent—things like societies, laws, cultures, arts, civilizations, all the products of human artifice. But life is not an artifice. Life is not man-made. We did not create or invent life, our lives, ourselves. If there is a meaning to our very lives and our very selves, it must be there by nature, not by art; or, saying the same thing in a different way, it must be objective, not subjective; or, saying the same thing again in a third way, it must be by divine art, not human art, God-made, not man-made. The meaning of life therefore requires a God.

The secularist can still maintain that many things in life have meanings, proximate meanings, relative meanings, man-made and therefore man-revisable meanings. But he can't maintain that life itself has meaning without appealing to the forbidden sector of reality (the supernatural) that his tiny, flattened philosophy will not allow him to enter. And because the secularist has only proximate and not ultimate meanings, relative but not absolute meanings, man-made and man-revisable but not eternal meanings, therefore his ethical principles are relative to changing situations and motives and societies. They are subjective and dependent on man, not objective and dependent on God and in the very nature of things.

How does all this apply to suffering? Some suffering is man-made; war, for instance. But much is not, at least not in any clear and obvious way. We are born in suffering and we die in suffering, whether we are warmongers or peacemongers. Man-made sufferings, like anything man-made, can have a meaning for the modern secular mind, but not non-man-made sufferings, not the sufferings inherent in life itself, not Virgil's *lacrimae rerum* (the tears of things), not Buddha's *dukkha* (alienation, suffering the gap between desire and reality). Once the divine author is declared to be dead, the characters in the human story can find no objective and ultimate meaning in their sufferings or in any other pervasive and natural feature of life like sex, which modernity also subjectivizes and trivializes.

3. Modernity's Forgetfulness of Heaven and Hell

"One world at a time," said Thoreau on his deathbed to the preacher who tried to get him to answer the most realistic question in the world: "Quo vadis?" Where are you going? Thoreau's is modernity's typical attitude, blindly sliding into the abyss and erecting billboards at the edge to look at, arranging deck chairs on the Titanic.

It was not always so. Every traditional society, every premodern society in history gave its people some other-worldly perspective on this world, saw this world as something like a womb, a way station, a wandering toward the next. And just as this world cuts two ways, just as there are little heavens and little hells here, so also there. The height of the mountain and the depth of the valley go together. The existence of some sort of heaven and some sort of hell colored the vision of our ancestors, but not of our contemporaries.

What difference does this fact make to the mystery of suffering? If there is a life after death and a heaven, then we can say with the apostle Paul, "I consider that the sufferings of this present time are not worth comparing with the glory that is to be revealed" (Rom 8:18). And if not, not. If there is no life after death, then suffering is an uncompensated loss, a scandal.

It is also a purposeless scandal. For if there is a life after death, suffering can have the profound meaning of birth pangs.

> When a woman is in travail she has sorrow, because her hour has come; but when she is delivered of the child, she no longer remembers the anguish, for joy that a child is born into the world. So you have sorrow now, but I will see you again and your hearts will rejoice, and no one will take your joy from you. (Jn 16:21-22)

But if there is no life after death, suffering is not birth pangs but only death pangs, echoes of the last and ultimate fact of nothingness reverberating back into all our years and draining from them color, meaning, and hope. If there is no heaven, death is spontaneous abortion.

Hell as well as heaven helps to explain suffering. Not all suffering is a way to God; some is a foretaste of hell. Suffering is a reflection of death, a reminder of mortality. Death, in turn, is punishment and consequence of sin. Sin, in turn, is the distant echo in our lives of hell. Hell's eternal and objective separation from God sends its ambassadors into our lives: repentable and volitional separations from God in the form of sins. Thus by a deathly chain, suffering is the remote echo of hell. Modernity cannot understand suffering very deeply because it does not believe in suffering's ultimate source. Hell, sin, and even death do not form a part of modernity's habitual vision of life.

4. Modernity's Forgetfulness of Solidarity

The twin mysteries of original sin and vicarious atonement are both rooted in the mystery of human solidarity. Original sin is solidarity in sin, vicarious atonement is solidarity in redemption. If modernity does not understand solidarity, it cannot understand original sin or vicarious atonement either. And these are two of the keys to unlocking the mystery of suffering.

The mystery of solidarity—what feelings spontaneously well up in us when we hear these two words? What prejudices must we overcome to look afresh? What tricks are being played on us by the little movie camera in our head that automatically flips up a picture whenever a word is sounded?

To modernity, *mystery* often connotes mystification, deliberate hiding of something. Or else a darkness, a negativity that is associated with horror movies and the occult. Or else, finally, a problem, an intellectual challenge, a puzzle to be solved by a detective. "A wonderful mystery" sounds to this mind almost like a square circle. But solidarity is a wonderful mystery.

Solidarity has a political connotation to modernity: something man-made and deliberate, and something external and visible. But the mystery of solidarity means something natural, not man-made, and something visible only to the inner eye of wisdom. It means that the human race is like a tree, or a vine, or a body: organically one. We see the different leaves and branches; we do not see the common sap or the common trunk.

All the mystery of solidarity is contained in the little word "in." No one but God has ever plumbed the depths of that word. Its depths are rooted in ultimate reality, in the Trinity, in the circumincession of the divine persons, the Father in the Son, the Son in the Father, both in the Spirit, the Spirit in both.

On the human level, the most profound story of solidarity ever written is Dostoyevski's *The Brothers Karamazov*. The central contrast of the story is between Alyosha, the solidarist, and his brother Ivan, who refuses this primal mystery. Two strange and wonderful principles of solidarity which Alyosha learns from Father Zossima are that each of us is really responsible for all of us, since we are our brothers' keepers and all men are our brothers; and that once we realize and accept this, we are already in paradise. Solidarity is heaven's earthly colony.

The eucharist is the ritual of solidarity: Christ in the Christian, the Christian in Christ. The worshipper is incorporated into Christ, into the sacrifice; he becomes one with it as he becomes one with food, since in the eucharist Christ's sacrifice is assimilated as food. And you are what you eat. "How very peculiar, as strange as can be: whatever Miss T eats turns into Miss T." In the eucharist Christ and Christian become one, heaven and earth become one. The mystery defies words; only "in" will do. Christ by his in-carnation incorporated or in-bodied humanity in-to his divinity, so that, when we are in-corporated into his body, his divinity is incorporated into our humanity. You have to read that sentence three or four times. I'm sorry, but there it is.

The eucharist is the solution to the problem of suffering. For it is the taking up of suffering into sacrifice. Human punitive suffering, the mark of mortality and sin, becomes one with divine redemptive suffering, the mark of eternal life and grace. (That's another sentence you have to read a few times.)

You do not understand this? Neither do I. Who does? We don't even understand love or loyalty or life. But that is no reason for refusing any of these gifts.

5. Modernity's Forgetfulness of Original Sin

"We suffer and die because Adam ate an apple. That makes no sense at all."

How about this one, then? Your children are born with AIDS because you contracted it by a blood transfusion when you were pregnant. Does that make sense?

Both seem unfair. Both seem to make no moral sense. But the second happens. Why couldn't the first?

The forbidden fruit, of course, had no magic to it. It was the disobedience to God that alienated Adam and Eve, not the fruit. The great divorce was made by their souls, not their bodies, by their choice to follow the snake instead of God. We've been crawling on our bellies ever since.

But how can God fairly punish us for Adam's sin? He doesn't. He punishes us for our own. But our own sin is conditioned by Adam's. We are not unconditioned, totally free, like God creating a world out of nothing. We create really free choices, all right, but not out of nothing. We create and choose out of something, out of conditioned factors in our world and in ourselves. We are given the blocks of marble out of which we sculpt; only God creates his own. Our environment is our world, and our heredity is our selves. Thus heredity and environment condition all our choices.

But since we are creatures of soul as well as body, and since we inherit our human nature from our parents, there is therefore spiritual heredity as well as physical. We inherit from our ancestors their proclivities and instincts and emotional patterns as well as their skin color and size. Original sin is the proclivity to say "my will be done" instead of "thy will be done." Once Adam and Eve tasted the independence and alienation and disobedience, they became disobedience addicts. That is what sin is, a spiritual addiction. Just as a dope addict can pass on his addiction to his children, so can sin addicts.

So it could have happened, just as Christian theology says. But is it fair? If not, then, as Ivan Karamazov concludes, the whole world is not fair. It is not fair that we have any influence for good over each other either, then; that we can carry each other's burdens, both physical and spiritual; that we can touch and influence each other at all. If we can touch each other (body or soul) for good, we can touch each other for evil too. If we can touch to love, we can also touch to kill. The price God had to pay to create a world in which we are free to love each other and to express that love in deed was a world in which we are also free to harm each other. Original sin *is* unfair, just as a baby inheriting a heroin addiction is unfair.

Fairness, or justice, is important—much more important than modernity thinks, as I shall try to argue in a few pages— but love is more important, and if God had to risk justice in order to guarantee love, that is what he did. (That is not the best way to put it; what he did was to satisfy both, to reconcile both.) But better that, better love and injustice than no love. Making us robots would have guaranteed justice but at the expense of love. God is just, but he is not justice itself. He is love itself. Justice is not God's essence. Love is God's essence. Justice is one of the attributes of love. Since God is love, he never will or can compromise love. Instead, to create a race capable of freely loving, he will risk injustice and consequent suffering, i.e., the kind of world we make by the wrong use of our freedom.

6. Modernity's Forgetfulness of Vicarious Atonement

"Where sin increased, grace abounded all the more" (Rom 5:20). Solidarity in sin is more than made up for by solidarity in salvation. "As in Adam all die, so also in Christ shall all be made alive" (1 Cor 15:22).

The modern mind no more understands how one man dying on a cross yesterday gets eternal life into my soul today and gets me into heaven tomorrow than it understands how Adam and Eve's apple picking expedition doomed all their children to death. The key in both cases is heredity. We are not born into this world as mere individuals but as parts of a family, a single worldwide human family. We tend to forget this. We are so rightfully concerned to avoid racism that we forget race, so concerned not to divide the human race racially that we forget that it is united racially. We are all Adam's children by physical birth; we can all become God's children by spiritual rebirth, by being "born from above" of water and the Spirit, i.e., by baptism and faith. (The two always go together in the New Testament; baptism is not external magic and faith is not internal musing; both are deed.)

Vicarious atonement means that what Christ did atones for our sin: "By his stripes we are healed." How this works, the spiritual technology God uses, no one knows. But it is based on a true principle, a law of human nature that everyone knows deep down though the modern mind has forgotten it. This is solidarity. We are "in" our new spiritual ancestor, Christ, as we were "in" our old physical ancestor Adam, in his loins, his genes. Once, the tree of humanity was only two twigs; from the first "two become one," we all grew. So, once upon a time the new tree of redeemed humanity was but one twig, Christ; from that twig we all grew, after being engrafted onto it by faith and baptism. "I am the vine, you are the branches," he says. Branches of the same vine. The very same life, like blood, flows through the vine and the branches.

Sexual reproduction and physical birth is the way the Adam-life is spread. Faith and baptism is the way the Christ-life is spread. Both ways are surprises. Little children often refuse to believe the real answer to the question, "Where did I come from?" The stork seems more reasonable. The new life fits this pattern of a wonderful and mysterious surprise. We should not be surprised that it is surprising.

When E.T. (the extra-terrestrial) landed outside Detroit,

Henry Ford III took him on a tour of his auto factory. "What do you make here?" E.T. asked. "Cars." "That's amazing!" said E.T. "Why," asked Henry Ford, "don't you have factories on your planet too?" "Oh, yes. But we make babies in our factories. How do you make babies on earth?" Henry told him, and E.T. said, "That's amazing! That's how we make cars."

Vicarious atonement is Christ's surprising solution to suffering. He destroys suffering by suffering! He drains the sin, death, and eventually suffering out of the world like a blotter, or a toilet bowl. He stoops to the lowest place, the place the sediment sinks to.

But we still suffer, you object. Ah, but only for a little while. Christ's work won for us a world free of suffering because free of sin, a world called heaven, or God's house, God's family mansion. We are presently beginning our preparation, or purification, or purgatory, if you will, our training. Yes, our toilet training. We are only spiritual babies, and we are learning some of the elementary ways of that house, and learning very slowly. We have to take many scalding hot baths (a painful process) to wash the dirt off. But the bathroom (purgatory, if you will) is already part of the mansion (heaven). If we are in Christ, we are already in paradise.

Christ promised the dying thief on the cross, "Today you shall be with me in paradise." Yet Christ did not ascend into heaven until forty days later. The explanation of the puzzle is, I think, that where Christ is, there is paradise. Heaven doesn't make Christ Christ; Christ makes heaven heaven. Heaven does not make its inhabitants heavenly; they make it heaven. The same is true of places on earth: people make places more than places make people. "It takes a heap of living to make a house a home." The psalm says of Christ's people, "as they go through the valley of Baca they make it a place of springs" (Ps 84:6). Even in the desert of our suffering, our spirit smiles in hope and in assurance, even if our face is grimacing with pain. For we know where we are and whose we are:

I also suffer these things; nevertheless I am not ashamed, for I know Whom I have believed and am persuaded that He is able to keep what I have committed to Him until that Day. (2 Tm 1:12, NKJV)

By means of vicarious atonement, the tears of Job become the tears of Jesus.

7. *Modernity's Forgetfulness of Justice*

Here is a very good question: If suffering is punishment for sin, why can't God just not punish us, if he's so loving? The governor can pardon a justly condemned criminal; why can't God just step in with a pardon? Why does Christ have to die? Why must anyone die? Why must anyone suffer?

To answer this question we must go back to a fundamental idea, the idea of justice. Modernity asks this question because it does not understand justice. To the modern mind, justice means what ought to be, an ideal. But justice is also something that is. To the modern mind, justice exists in the mind, or in the will, which has ideals and makes laws. But justice also exists before, above, and outside all human minds and wills. It is objective, cosmic, necessary, and absolute. That is why we can say some human laws are not just: because there is this higher standard, an objective standard, God's standard. "If God did not exist, everything would be permissible," says Dostoyevski. The modern mind says that only human laws make things not permissible. "If it feels good, do it." "If it doesn't hurt anybody, why not?" "If society approves, then it's O.K."

This is absurd, of course. It would mean that we would have absolutely no justification for opposing tyranny, genocide, racism, suicide, abortion, or any other barbarity if only that barbarity were ensconced in law. It would mean that war and force were the only way to settle disputes between two different societies with two different sets of laws (a conclusion

Hegel happily affirms). It would mean that when a parent says to a child, "You shouldn't do that," he could mean only, "I don't like it when I see you do that." It would mean that an evil deed is no more than an evil taste.

The alternative philosophy of justice, the philosophy of objective, cosmic, divine justice, means that justice is unchangeable and never to be gotten around. It means that our previous explanation of God setting justice aside for the sake of something higher, love, is incorrect. Love is higher than justice, as geometry is higher than arithmetic, but "the highest does not stand without the lowest" (C.S. Lewis). Cosmic justice is not like man-made justice, a set of rules that we can set aside like the rules of a game or the laws of a state. Rather, justice is like mathematics: eternal, unchangeable, and necessary. Two plus two can never be five.

There are in fact three levels of laws, and justice is on top, in the most necessary and unexceptional kind of all. On the lowest of the three levels are man-made laws, which are changeable at will. Next come God-made physical laws, like gravity. These don't change, but they can. Miracles can set them aside. And they could have been different to begin with; God could have created a different kind of physical universe, e.g., with three kinds of electrical charges instead of two. Highest of all are laws that not even God can change, because they are based on the nature of God. These include metaphysical laws, laws of being, e.g., that being is not non-being; that there must be a cause or sufficient reason for every being that comes into being; that all being is intelligible or true and knowable by omniscience. They also include logical laws, e.g., that $x=x$ and $x \neq$ non-x; that a thing is itself and is not what it isn't; and that if all A is B and all B is C, then all A is C. Even miracles do not contradict logic. Jesus may walk through walls, but he does not both walk through walls and not walk through walls at the same time. He may turn water into wine, but if his water is wine and if wine is red, then that water-turned-to-wine is red. Thirdly, there are mathematical laws. Miracles also do not violate them. If five loaves fed five thousand people, that means they fed a thousand times as much as five people. Fourthly, and finally, ethical laws are also in this category of the unchangeable. Justice remains justice though all men should act or think unjustly. Modernity places justice into the lowest category, the man-made. Traditional Christian theology places it into the highest, for it is an attribute of God.

From that point of view, Christ's saving us is not really like the prison chaplain stepping up to go to the electric chair so that the prisoner can go free. For the prisoner does not have to die. The law could be changed. The governor could pardon the prisoner, if he were merciful enough. And God, the governor of the universe, is more merciful than any. But justice demands payment. Christ's salvation is more like someone interposing himself between a bullet and a victim. The only way to save the victim is to be the victim. Christ interposes his body between ours and the divine lightning of justice. The lightning strikes him instead. We made ourselves incapable of enduring the divine lightning, the truth. Someone has to endure the truth. It's us or him. The good news is that it's him. But the good news, the gospel, makes no sense without justice, without somebody having to endure it.

Once the lightning bolt of truth and justice is shot out from heaven, there's no stopping it. We decided to build our house upon the sand and to build it of wood and hay and stubble. Lightning would destroy such a house. The only way to save us is for Christ to tie himself to our house as a lightning rod and take the lightning bolt himself. The incarnation is his tying himself to our humanity; his death is his taking the bolt of justice. The bolt is unstoppable. Modernity does not see that, therefore does not understand why he has to suffer or why we do.

In sum, there's good news and bad news. The bad news is

that "the wages of sin is death." That's justice. The good news is that "the gift of God is eternal life in Christ Jesus our Lord." That's grace.

A Last Word

Reader: I see . . .

Author: Do you?

Reader: Well, I'm not sure I see the realities you see, but I see the idea, the picture that you're painting.

Author: That's not enough.

Reader: It's more than I expected. You delivered much more than you promised, you know. You promised only an answer to the problem of suffering, and you delivered a picture that really includes the whole Christian thing.

Author: If it didn't convince you, it's less, not more, than I had hoped. And I didn't promise an answer to the problem of suffering, only an exploration of the mystery of suffering. And my picture didn't include the whole of Christianity either; there's much, much more. But in a sense, yes, it's the whole. Because it's a picture, and in a picture you have to have the whole in order to understand any of the parts. They're organically related, as in a body. An answer to the mystery of suffering taken out of the whole picture would be like an eye or an ear taken out of a body and put on a plate. Something of "the whole Christian thing" has to come along with the answer to suffering, as the rest of the body comes along with an ear. But it's not even a picture; that analogy isn't strong enough. It's a person. It's him.

Reader: You can't give me him.

Author: Oh, I know that. But the picture is a picture of him. It's meant to lead beyond itself to him, to point him out, like John the Baptist.

Reader: Still, it's only a picture.

Author: Do you believe it's true?

Reader: I don't know.

Author: You can say both "I don't know" and "I believe," you know.

Reader: I can believe now, if I want to. I'll say that much. You made it intellectually credible.

Author: Do you realize what's left then?

Reader: Yes. The will. Will I accept this God who lets me and my loved ones suffer? Will I trust him that he's doing it for love, not out of spite or indifference?

Author: That is precisely the question. Now it's between you and him. I've done my work. Goodbye.

Reader: Goodbye. Thank you for clearing away some of the obstacles on the intellectual road.

Author: That's what apologists are: street sweepers.

*　　*　　*

Our journey of exploration down the long, winding river of tears began with some hard questions. In trying to give some answers, we have not eliminated questions; we are left with both questions and answers. We should not be afraid of either. Conservatives often seem afraid of questions and liberals afraid of answers—which is even sillier, because that's like being afraid of food. Being afraid of questions is like being afraid of hunger. That's only cowardice.

The answers we found were first some clues. The Bible too seems full of clues. And the words of Jesus most of all. They are true and profound, but they are pointers that we have to follow; they should not end our quest, any more than marriage should end courtship. Our answers were, in the second place, more like parts of a picture, a vision, than parts of a puzzle or the conclusion of an equation. And in the third place, the picture was a moving picture, a story, and we are in that story. Chesterton says somewhere that the only two things that never get boring are a person and a story, and even a story has to be about a person. Fourth and most important of all, our answer turned out to be a person, one who fulfilled the clues, capstoned the picture, and climaxed the story.

When we begin to understand the significance of the Man of

Sorrows, sorrow and suffering seem far less threatening to us than they do at first. Indeed, when history is seen as his-story, suffering is seen as the dark spot in a magnificent painting, heard as the low note in a harmony whose high notes are lost in heaven, a dance descending in cascades of eucatastrophe from archangels to a stable, through a cross to an empty tomb and back to heaven with the promise that he will also empty the tombs of ourselves, our children, and our ancestors.

> Then I saw a new heaven and a new earth; for the first heaven and the first earth had passed away, and the sea was no more. And I saw the holy city, new Jerusalem, coming down out of heaven from God, prepared as a bride adorned for her husband; and I heard a loud voice from the throne saying, "Behold, the dwelling of God is with men. He will dwell with them, and they shall be his people, and God himself will be with them; he will wipe away every tear from their eyes, and death shall be no more, neither shall there be mourning nor crying nor pain any more, for the former things have passed away." And he who sat upon the throne said, "Behold, I make all things new." Also he said, "Write this, for these words are trustworthy and true." (Rv 21:1-5)

Those who believe the man who made these and other incredible promises are called Christians. Life's greatest adventure is to be one.

Other Books of Interest
by Peter Kreeft

Making Choices
Practical Wisdom for Everyday Moral Decisions

"It's a moral jungle out there," writes Peter Kreeft. In *Making Choices,* he describes why we find decision-making so difficult and living with our choices even harder. With penetrating wisdom, good humor, and common sense, Peter Kreeft draws a map through the everyday jungle or moral choices, one simple enough for the believer and convincing enough for the skeptic.

Making Choices is a powerful aid for all who desire clarity when facing decisions, certitude when making them, and happiness when living with their consequences. *$8.99*

The God Who Loves You
Knowing the Height, Depth,
and Breadth of God's Love for You

Only when you begin to know God as a lover knows the beloved does everything else begin to make sense, insists Peter Kreeft. Only then does Scripture, world history, and your own life experience come into focus as God's continuing love story.

When you discover afresh the true meaning of God's love and its impact on your relationship with him and others, it becomes clearer how love solves every problem and satisfies the deepest yearnings of the heart. Originally published as *Knowing the Truth of God's Love.* *$8.99*

Available at your Christian bookstore or from:
Servant Publications · Dept. 209 · P.O. Box 7455
Ann Arbor, Michigan 48107
Please include payment plus $2.75 per book
for postage and handling.
*Send for our FREE catalog of Christian
books, music, and cassettes.*